The Love Riddle

by

Eithne Strong

Attic Press
DUBLIN

First published in Ireland in 1993 by
Attic Press
4 Upper Mount Street
Dublin 2

British Library Cataloguing in Publication Data
Strong, Eithne
The Love Riddle
I. Title
823.914 [F]

ISBN 1 85594 084 1

Cover Design: Kate White
Photo: Justin Elliott
Origination: Verbatim Typesetting and Design
Printing: The Guernsey Press Co Ltd

This book is published with the assistance of The Arts Council/An Chomhairle Ealaíon.

DELETED

Dedication

To life

About the Author

Eithne Strong, poet in Irish and English, is also a fiction writer. A varied life includes taking a university degree after family rearing, participating in publishing, freelance journalism, teaching, work with the media, co-ordinating creative writing courses, giving readings of her work widely and representing Irish writing in Europe—Denmark, France, Germany, Finland—in England, the USA and Canada. She has been awarded travel bursaries. Her work appears in many anthologies. She is a member of the executive committee of the Irish Writers' Union.

Born in West Limerick, she has lived for many years in Dublin where she was married, had nine children and was widowed. She has been involved with the mentally disabled—her youngest son has a mental disability.

Thirteen of Eithne Strong's books have been published.

One

'Find an heiress, Nelson, who will swoon with love for you. Enslave her. Marry her for all our sakes.'

His mother's joke. But, of course, also her wish.

Nelson had told Una about this on the side of Glencree in the early summer of 1942. It was now November down in the city. Icy. Shrill.

In Cornwall it was more wildly so. There, at this moment, his mother, Mrs Paul Forterre, was thinking of him. Her darling sonny. She couldn't understand him. He had taken up with that Penn Reade who influenced him still further away, although in his letters Nelson insisted that he was close, concerned, more than ever he had been. It was true that in the years since he had followed that man from Manchester to Dublin he had written regularly, had never forgotten her birthday. But she could no longer understand him. Nor could the others in the family.

She was in the tiny stone cottage that had been found for her in a pocket off the coast when the evacuation took effect. Alone, geographically removed from kith and kin, oppressed within the lunatic hurricane, she thought about all the money that had been lost through Paul's investments. Her amiable, luckless Paul who devotedly ministered to his flock, who had so suddenly died, poor, leaving her poor, poor, in spite of the high titles in the network of relatives. Nelson was like his father in that: no aptitude for affairs. That odious Penn Reade was an incomprehensible influence. Nelson, aligning himself with the man's intolerable ideas, would not make money. Perhaps it had never been in Nelson to do so. Making money seemed to have gone out with Great-uncle von Kleber. There were those in the family affiliations on Paul's side who affected to despise the business of money-making, the preoccupation of Jews. There had been times when she'd felt it necessary to veil aspects of her origins. And the German cousins still left in their wretched country—unfortunate creatures, one worries dreadfully for them these days. Were they even there at all any more? No letters for ages.

She had her old fur coat—generations old—as a rug about her fragile knees. She pulled it closer and poked, just a very little, the low fire.

'I *will* build shelters for your head,' Nelson said to Una.

Put in the plural like that and with the emphasis on 'will', it affected her. Ten minutes previously she had been ashamed of him. His coat, originally an expensive dark woollen garment, now third time handed on—uncle to father to Nelson—was greying and frayed at the seams. For him, at this time, to say he would build shelters for her head was crazy—and touching. His shoes needed heeling; on his head was an out-of-place old shooting cap, another heirloom. To say such a thing was romantic. At nineteen, hearing it comforted her in spite of all the other things. His coat collar was turned up as far as it would go against the north wind tearing up the Liffey. On the days when he went to his part-time work in the office of the printing firm, his detachable shirt collar showed white, freshly clean. A laundered collar, daily, that had been a maxim of family training; he adhered to it selectively. He had jettisoned so many of the maxims but, for the job, he had considered clean neckwear a necessary expenditure out of the three pounds a week wage. Yet today it did not show. Nor for the past week had there been its white evidence of employment. The printing firm needed him no longer. Cutbacks. A part-timer was the first to go.

He had affirmed quietly, as they forged along by the wintry wall of Eden Quay, that he would build shelters for her head. He meant it.

The part-time job, anyway, had been a favour created because of some tenuous family connection. The family connections ramified through continental Europe, England—his native place, Scotland, Wales, and even touched in the lightest way a nerve or two in Ireland. He had told her he liked the antiquity of their beginnings. He disliked asking favours but his dislike fought with a belief he had come to have in the correctness of interdependence. His need had been great, the scholarship and odd newspaper work not being enough to see him through the degree course he had taken up so late at Trinity.

Una walked beside him as he pushed her bicycle along the pavement across O'Connell Bridge. She knew he believed, at this his lowest financial point, returning from the dole queue, that he would build shelters for her head. The shame of that, the dole queue. At home in Balnahown the dole was amongst the lowest disgraces. She could hear what would be said if they knew.

'Bad luck was bound to follow what you did,' Minnie would say and much more.

'Just so, God knows, just so.' Sean's forehead would ridge with a confusion of pressures. He and Minnie did not know what to make of their daughter. Their common affliction at her conduct making them a little more aproachable to each other, they would speak together of how Jack, who had heart-scalded them with his lackadaisical progress at the university, had even so never done a retrograde thing as his sister had done. Jack himself was altogether furious with her. That showed he was sound in faith, they would say, the Lord would surely bless his loyalty, set him right in the next step after the finals.

Una had waited in a doorwway, rooted in shame, pretending to have nothing to do with Nelson standing in the down-and-out line. She was angry with her shame; with him for being in so stricken a condition—didn't his family and he himself, sometimes, in spite of his disavowals, bolster themselves up with reference to a proud lineage. She was angry with their love, that mutual plight of emotion which tangled them together in this penurious state; angry with the firm that needed him no longer.

He repeated it once again. This time however she squeezed his left hand inside the sopping glove.

'That's my girl.'

He had told her that when he was a child they had been greatly troubled at his stubbornness. This was amongst the many things he told her on the side of Glencree in the weeks after they had first met, six months previously in May 1942. When he was a grown young man, his mother and nanny, both, had given him instances of their earliest distress on his account. To gain his own way, they said, he would hold his breath until his face began to go blue. His mother could not handle the situation. The first time it happened, Nanny said, his mother fainted. Nanny had to throw cold water over him to bring him out of his blue face.

Sleet beat at them mercilessly. Her legs were purple. Her knees ached with cold. She wished fur-lined trousers were in fashion and that she could afford a pair. As it was, she possessed no leg covering apart from two pairs of anklesocks. She had stuffed the spare pair into one pocket of her gaberdine coat the morning she cycled away after Minnie and Sean had left for the school. In the other pocket she had crammed the hunk of brown bread grabbed from the kitchen against the journey.

Jack had said he would swing for an Englishman. Nelson's sister had written, 'What is she? Is she one of us or is she of the lower orders?'

'Why?' Lady Duncarty had asked him in her residence beyond the Phoenix Park, 'Why ever did you come in the first place? Shouldn't you now be with our boys out there in the thick of it? Are you not a war-dodger?'

He had received no further invitations from her.

He had come with introductions to some high places. Being 'one of us' incorporated the instilled, the reflexive observation of certain elitist rules and attitudes, many idiotically petty in their separatist implementing, quite ridiculously exacting the oddest requirements such as leaving unfastened the bottom waistcoat button, always replying to How do you do? with precisely the same formula, and so on and on. Before he came and since, he had spent much time stubbornly examining and testing against life the thinking, the rules into which he had been born. Penn

Reade's way of thinking, he said to Una, made sense for him. Largely because it did, he himself had come to reject much of what upbringing had insisted was essential. He had rejected the support of war. To do this at a time when your country was engaged in a terrible conflict, while in the name of being allowed, was in reality seen as treachery. Pacifists and conscientious objectors were cads, bounders, traitors posing as enlightened thinkers.

To reject the establishment in any of its entrenched structures, so as to seek out more open values, was to be in peril. To have nothing materially secure. This, however, was his choice.

In his shabby handed-on tweeds and flannels, his worn leather patches on the elbows, his elegantly elocuted vowels and consonants, his concepts of peace and dedication where were machinations of world war abroad and at home hatchings of reprisals, vengeance, violent reappropriation of stolen counties, Una believed she saw and heard a new animal. Worth some attention. Much attention.

The man who, for the present, was earning a meagre sum patrolling the turf stacks to forestall thieves in Phoenix Park, and whom they knew from the Friday evenings at the Reades' house, had cycled with her until she saw Nelson in the dole queue. The man had then gone on to his work. Since what had come to be referred to as 'the abduction'—the merest trace of a smile in the reference to take from the unhappiness—someone always accompanied her. Nelson and she now went into Trinity so that he could collect his bicycle from its locked stand there. He cycled with her the six miles back to the Reades' home, still unsure if it was safe for her to be alone anywhere outside that house.

Love is sustained volition and action, willing the good, carrying it out. That was what Penn Reade said the first time she went to one of the Friday evenings. What did she think, Nelson wanted to know afterwards as they cycled to her digs. Nothing new in that anyway, she said. Wasn't it the same as Love thy neighbour as thyself, just put differently. But of course there had been new things, as well. Very new. They held her; she went back each week with Nelson from then on. Listening, questioning. Beatrice Reade was a quiet woman, gracious to all who came. She probably knew a lot about sustained volition and action for what was good. Her husband was not an easy person, probably often difficult to live with in close proximity. He said so himself. Ask Beatrice if I'm worth it, he added. Wasn't this enormous egotism? On the other hand there was something enviable in such assurance of expression, not caring what anyone listening thought. Madeline Reade did not like Una's staying in the house these last months. If anything to do with the 'abduction' came up in her hearing, her mouth took on a twist that with no sound said Piffle! Madeline did not like many things that her father instigated. She would like to reinvent her father.

Mrs Forterre got up from the chair lifting, as she did so, the old fur coat on to the table nearby. It became more difficult all the time to unfold oneself. Too horrific a storm today to venture beyond the door. But one must exercise if only round and round the interior. She went to the little back porch to fetch further fuel. Damp logs. As she set it down she caught a sideways view of herself in the wall mirror, Something made her take a second look. Full front. Grey. Everything on me is grey. Hair. I had such wonderful hair. Is my skin also going grey? I refuse to be grey all over. Even if no one is likely to come near me for days. There *will* be colour.

She pulled a crimson scarf from a drawer over her shoulders and shaped it softly under her chin. One thing about the cottage is that all one's things are so close to hand. You stretch out a finger and there they are. A blessing. That scarf is an improvement. I do still have vestiges of handsomeness. I can look a hag as well. I refuse to be a grey hag—today anyway. I could of course change tomorrow. I dread the tomorrows...dark, dark...lonely...I must not think too much about the dismal side of Nelson's behaviour. There is much good in him. If only that Penn Reade...

In May 1942 Nelson had said, 'Academically, the wife is highly regarded...'

'Wife?'

'Oh that's just the way it's said here—the chap who shares rooms with you is called your wife, just colllege stuff.'

'Never heard such a thing!'

'Anyway he has several scholarly works to his name. He doesn't like women. We're like chalk and cheese.'

'I'll keep out of his way.'

'Oh he won't be coming here just now—it's not that he'd be rude, nothing so obvious, it's just that women are not his line. He's never here very much, really; stews in the library or keeps concourse with his cronies when he's not lecturing. Mostly here for breakfast; drops his crusts all over the floor, Not too keen on washing of the person either. You could say he prides himself in being the eccentric academic.'

'Why did you choose him as your...wife?'

'I didn't. He was here before me. The rooms are ours by courtesy of Professor Bramer who doesn't use them except to keep a corner of the study. Pops in every now and then with books and papers and so on, that's all. Very decent of him to offer me the other room: rooms are scarce. I count myself very lucky here, much more space than in Botany Bay.'

Nelson had asked her to lunch for the first time. Porridge. Cheap. Nutritious. Twenty minutes on the lowest flame, he said. A single gas ring with a dispirited long rubber pipe. Boiling the kettle had to wait until the porridge was ready. She had brought sugar buns from Johnston, Mooney & O'Brien in Leinster Street.

'Bad for you,' he said, 'give you pimples. Porridge is wholesome. I eat it with a little salt. Going back to my nursery days you'll say, I suppose, when I tell you it was constant daily fare set before us by our Scottish nanny.'

'Nanny? You had a nanny?'

'Nanny Cairn.'

'I've come across nannies only in stories. There could not be two more different backgrounds than yours and mine.'

'Good, that's good. Contrast is the stuff of progress—no progress without contrarieties, as Blake puts it.'

'So maybe you and your—your wife will progress

together?'

'Maybe. I'm working on my patience—and possibly he is on his. Nothing remotely of a personal nature is said between us, a civilised distance maintained. A bit more humour from each of us would be valuable—I'm short of it where he's concerned and his cold jokes are of a mathematical bent.'

'I've to be back at my desk very soon,' Una said.

'And I to mine. It takes me ten minutes on the bike up the quays with luck.'

'Lucky my Department is so near Trinity.'

'Glad you said that, maybe you'll be encouraged to come again. We must always finish with something raw—here, piece of carrot. You will come again?'

'Next time I'll bring an apple—with the pimply buns.'

'Apple in May? In wartime?'

'Well, we'll see—anyway, I notice people in Dublin mostly call it the Emergency—but I can always find dandelion leaves, really fresh. But you wouldn't eat those.'

'Try me. Lunchtime it has to be—women all have to be out by six. It can be six often before I get back here.'

'Another one of those boys-all-gang-together places.'

'It looks that way, I'm afraid.'

'A whole crowd of Jacks: my brother Jack would never let me into any of his doings—until very lately.'

'When will you tell me about Jack?'

'Ah Jack…I've always been bothered one way and another about Jack.'

'Jack…you'll tell me…and about other things…

maybe? Some time? We could cycle up to the hills on a Saturday, a fine Saturday? A good place to talk, the hills?'

'I love the hills. That would be great.'

Two

So on a Saturday in May 1942, a fine day in the hills, Una commenced.

'It will be bits and pieces. Jigsaw. It will be that way.'

'Yes,' he said, 'for me too...we'll make pictures.'

In the beginning was the jiggle of a rhyme—sugar and spice and all things nice. It maddened Jack. And Una sang it at him over and over. She was weary of it. It wasn't true anyway: there were smelly girls, greasy women. But it infuriated Jack. Her only power over him was to enrage him. She deeply loved him. She longed for him to even like her.

Oh the paralysing cold! To have to wake up to that. It was surely around nine for that was daylight in spite of all the thick ice shapes darkening the glass. A wonder they hadn't called him yet.

'Hurry up Jack. Ja-ack...' His father. The second call a lot louder than the first. Before the door slammed on it. That was Una's slam. Letting him know she was to the fore. The parents never had to call her. She was always up.

Acute embarrassment. That was what Jack felt in regard to his family. They didn't often visit him in Tubbernagur. All of eighty miles. It took the entire day for them to get there and back, so they could spend only a very little part of it with him. In spite of the agonies of homesickness, he felt it was maybe just as well, the scarcity of their visits. His mother would wear one of those terrible hats, bad enough when she bought it and hideous by the time she had finished fiddling around with it, tricking it up. Never would she leave a hat alone. His father, in his Dripsey tweed, would keep saying ah no ah no or else thanks thanks thanks to the people in authority if they got over their meanness enough to offer refreshments. Why couldn't his father relax and be like he was when standing at the edge of the moor, looking away across it? And there was the horror of Una, uglier than ever now with the goggles. Having to traipse around the grounds with all that on view. Spot the Normiles, fellas! Did you ever...and so forth. What a great relief it would be to exist without the embarrassments of family. And yet....

If only they wouldn't urge him so much.

'Ja-ack, Jack...'

There was a lot he wanted to do if only they would just let him go his own way. But they urged their way in spite of the pneumonia two years running in that terrible place. All due allowances made, they said, for the way he could get run down. Didn't they send him, parcel post, certain foods. They paid, hard though it was, for some extras at the college, an orange a day, cod-liver oil, cocoa at night.

'Come on, Jack, stir yourself.'

Soon the footsteps would be coming up the stairs. Outside it was freezing hard. From his bed against the east wall, he brought himself to look again at the ice patterns on the window. It took a lot to get up and face what that meant. It took heat. There was none. The wall by his bed met the merciless east wind. The beige linoleum, with big blue unbelievable roses at the corners, kept lifting off the floor from the draught through the boards. Yes, it took a lot, it took time, especially; time to try yet again to gather a bit of courage to square up to the unrelenting fact that it was the skinning January morning when he must go back to that rotten place. To square up to their expectations. They wanted him to shine. Entirely for his own good, they said. He had all the brains a person could wish, lucky not to have been born like Dinny Doyle, Lord preserve us! You don't value your luck, Jack. Bone lazy. Given a good head and making no effort where it is most needed.

There was no time. 'Hurry, hurry Jack, finish your trunk. The books! Don't you know you'll be murdered without the maths books. And don't let me ever see a mark like that again. Disgrace! Idler!'

His room was a shambles. They all said it. 'Missis, I don't know what to do with Jack's room.'

'Leave it, Maggie, leave it. When he's gone to Tubbernagur we'll give it a good clean out.'

He didn't want them poking through his stuff. Left to himself, he knew where things were. They interfered. And every time he came home, things he valued were missing.

May–June 1942. Nelson and Una. The questions, the telling went on between them, when there was time. He had little of it: there were the lectures, the texts to be got through, the other demands the course involved; the part-time work. He also wrote freelance articles.

'I'll tell you, you'll tell me,' they said to each other. On the streets, in the hills, the parks, his rooms, by the sea. He said his telling would take longer, he had twelve years extra to account for. Porridge, dandelion leaves, carrots, raw stuff, sugar buns—all part of it, he said. They could feed each other. She was beset with appetite, avid for the new. So much to be learned. He was looking into the matter of possible lectures, a course for her in the college. People, places, events, sensations, to travel, savour other cultures, get outside the bounds of the island—these, she said, she longed to experience. Twelve years older than her, sprung from totally different beginnings, all that much more experience, Nelson Forterre was a gateway. He was worth attention. Yet he too wanted to know: things only she could tell him, or so he said. He seemed to mean it. She was pleased he asked.

'Your father, tell me about him.'

'Any telling about him will have to have mixed in other people: my mother, and certainly more about Jack—Jack, of enormous importance to my parents, the firstborn, the boy, you see—he's the one who, taken for granted, is now getting the university course. Mind you, I don't grudge that but I'd make better use of it. As I said already, our stupid county council doesn't give scholarships or I'd be in there this minute along with him and that's for sure...'

'Yes, yes, I know—and maybe yet something here is not impossible ...here in Trinity.'

'Ah but the archbishop...'

'We'll see, we are seeing... In the meantime you were going to tell me more—your father...'

'I was saying that talking about Daddy means talking about other people—there is for example Peetie, who keeps the land going or anyway is supposed to. There's Maggie, the girl helping...and oh, other people...the Rydalls, the Deerings...oh so much.'

When you thought about it, in reality it couldn't

be that much, not in comparison to what you could imagine to be his far-flung goings-on. But he kept insisting. 'Come on, paint me pictures.'

'Well, we can both paint, can't we?'

Sean Normile worried perpetually. Apart from Jack and the farm, there was the whole business back at the school of which he was principal.

You couldn't be up to this latest inspector from the Department. Dammit, you had to have every detail seen to, your syllabus clear-cut, a record of everything.

No matter what, Sean made sure to have his in good order, locking himself away from family distractions, coming out only to ask Minnie questions which irritated her, about curricular fine points.

Hadn't she her own school programme, she bitterly enquired of him, to keep up to date and run the house as well, seeing to the upkeep of everyone's clothes, seeing to it that Maggie swept under the beds, that she didn't lapse over the chopped nettles to the hens and didn't waste at every turn. In reply to his fiddle faddle questions, she was wont to tell him that he couldn't boil water, that the four sisters, who reared him after their mother died at his birth, left him incapable of doing a hand's turn for himself. He expected to be looked after top to toe and then he had to bother her about *his* syllabus, *his* roll book, *his* averages when there was nothing to stop him getting on with it, locking himself away from all disturbances whenever he liked. Where and when could *she* do that? God knows, nowhere, ever.

For a long time now she had not addressed him as 'Sean' except in front of some visitors. Her doing so at these times made her family uncomfortable: they were used to her calling him 'Daddy'. She could put a great variation of feeling into the way she said that word.

He worried about the farm, also, although much less than about his responsibilities at the school. The farm was a hundred acres of poor land, bog and sedge. A few fields, with much encouragement, yielded hay; it meant arduous draining and manuring, but that failing, they reverted to rushes. And who was to see to the encouragement? That could not be left to Peetie on his own: he had to be told and then checked on. Word had to be sent for a helping man when the drains clogged and leaked, when the loads of topdress from the pile outside the cowshed had to be spread. There were dry cattle to be herded from one patch of grazing to another; cows to be taken to the bull.

Schoolmaster Normile had to think of these things; he found it very difficult to put his mind to such details. In fact it was Minnie who urged him to them. Ostensibly, she did not want to have anything to do with farm matters: hadn't she enough on her hands, she repeated endlessly. Indeed, she seemed to wish to convey a certain aloofness from the land— she had been accustomed to the town only, before her post in the little country school. She did not traverse the Normile fields, unlike her family who, each with individual bent, never tired of doing so; she had not been even a single time around the full extent of the hilly boggy farm and said this every so often, sometimes with what seemed like a perverse pride. However, if she suspected Peetie was lurking in some obscure cover, indulging in idleness, she would say to her husband, 'Shouldn't that potato pit be dug, well before the frost?' or 'What about the glen meadow? I didn't see any topdress going down there yet.' And so on.

It was she and Maggie who kept tally of the calving dates, writing them down after the cows came from the bull. The record was pencilled on the back of the big calendar advertising Neary's General Grocery & Hardware. There was a rushed hugger-mugger to this setting down of dates if Jack or Una happened to come near while it was in progress, especially now that they were older. When they were younger, they got short answers to questions about cows and bulls and those dates, and other matters that all seemed part of inexplicable daily embarrass-ments, mystifications. Next to the calendar on the kitchen wall was a picture of the Virgin Mary.

The truth behind Sean Normile's worry regarding the farm was that he would have liked it to operate in its small way with the least possible expenditure of energy on his part. In spite of forbears who tilled and herded, he was no born farmer. Yet the land was essential for him—not primarily as a source of income, for there was little monetary profit in it although the fresh vegetables and the turf were prized benefits—but as another source.

Frequently he could be seen at different points on it, standing quite still and remaining that way for a long time. He was to be seen thus more certainly on Sundays or evenings having returned from the school where, a couple of hours previously, his bellows of frustration at particularly exasperating pupils were to be heard through the open windows of fine weather. Very often, just before twilight, he paced up and down the level stretch of boreen leading immediately off the yard. Having done this and finished his pipe, he went up to the rise of ground where the boreen stopped at the iron gate that gave on to the bye-road. From this rise, the land that was his, bounded by other holdings of moor and hill, was to be seen spreading away in the great variety of light and shade characteristic of the district. As twilight came on, there was often an immense stillness. He remained standing there until the night had settled in.

He worried about Jack, clever and making no right use of his brains. Instead of availing of the coaching he so ardently sought to implement upon him through the holidays, Jack did everything to dodge it.

Concocting clay heads from the blue mud out of the riverbank, making a mock of people. Science adventures, manufacturing bombs from God knows what, exploding the ditches. Drawing cartoons. Making a mock of people. No realisation whatever of the strain all that extra work of coaching was on a father who was himself supposed to be on holiday, gathering some strength for the grinding months ahead trying to put a bit of basic education into the heads of the sons of other people.

When Sean considered these things, the thought of Minnie's extra labours, particularly at turf and hay saving and the Christmas season, did not somehow come into his mind.

The Lord knows, it's very hard when your own son doesn't respond. Maths very important for boys. He's going to need those maths, the medical student he's supposed to be heading into is going to need maths. There have we been, scraping and saving from the beginning for the fees. But he's showing no signs of effort. Except for his own kind of inventions and experiments. Out in the shed or down the glen in that dugout—explode-out—he's made, or his room which is a sight. Maybe they're pointing to professional chemistry, science, these vagaries of his, and that would be hopeful—he'll find out for himself the need for mathematical exactness, precision. As for that other stuff, the crazy drawings, the mud creatures, all right for fun. Fun only. No future in that sort of stuff. He'd want to harden himself up, too. All right to be a reader, but not to be a mollycoddle at it. But then maybe the pneumonia two years running…True, he likes a bit of fishing. But no interest in doing any jobs on the land.

It struck Sean at this point that he and his son shared a certain reluctance to working the land. Laziness was the real word but not the quality to be squarely acknowledged with reference to himself. Were he to think further along the things he and Jack had in common, he might have found that, in truth, what they both most wished was a little steady money coming in without much effort on their part, to allow themselves the pursuit of what most pleased them. Sean did not allow such indulgent fantasy. His son did.

Three

May–June 1942

His mother, Nelson said, had had glorious hair. She had jokes and music and song. She laughed with visitors and made them laugh; she got him laughing too. That was when he was very young. Nanny Cairn dosed him—an entirely odious procedure—scrubbed him, smacked him to enforce good behaviour. Mummy called him 'My darling sonny.' He saw her hair in all its abundance and length when Nanny sometimes let him run to her in his nightshirt to say good morning. In his memory of them, these mornings seemed to be always in summer. His mother would be at her dressing-table, impatient at such a mass of springing hair; the sun would show all its different shades of chestnut and gold.

'My darling sonny, come and give me a big morning kiss.'

And he did, jumping on to her lap. But it was for only the briefest time he could remain there.

'Run along to Nanny now. I have to pin up and be in my best for the parish as soon as soon.'

It was a kind of joke: to be in her 'best for the parish' could mean any kind of occasion when she had to meet people, an actual parish event, but also a social engagement—luncheon, dinner, theatre up in London, or a weekend stay with a family connection. Yet the parish—the living went with the estate of a cousin, his father's cousin—was truly a matter to which she gave conscientious attention. She really stretched herself to meet the requirements of a clergyman's wife.

Nelson said he loved her with a great love. That word he never spoke. As a young boy, it seemed to him she was the dispenser of laughter. And of good things at tea when he and the others—two others—were sometimes allowed down from the nursery to join the grown-ups. Nanny Cairn saw to their bowels, their bath, their constant round of cleansing, exercise and good manners. Nelson repeated what he had told Una already, that when he held his breath in unutterable rage and went purple, she threw cold water over him to shock him out of such wickedness. His mother was not summoned after the first manifestation for on that occasion she had collapsed, managing first to exhale helplessly, 'Nanny, you must cope.' The recalcitrance of her children she could never handle without Nanny. The strictures for the shaping of their required mores she was incapable of enforcing unaided.

When Una asked, he said the family connections were, yes, a reality. There were—he deprecated—family trees ...

'Our mothers,' Una said, 'could not be more different.'

Jack still there. Trunk not yet ready for Peetie to take on ahead. No room for it in the Ford.

However cold it could be, he greatly valued his room. It had always been his. In the winter holidays, Minnie sometimes brought in the portable paraffin heater but the last few days no more oil. Gap in supplies. Could sometimes happen in the hard weather. He had a special feeling about his room, a feeling that was particularly powerful this morning while he still lay there in the bed, knowing time was running short. He'd like a bit more space, just. In fact, given his head and a steady little income requiring no effort, he would have three or four spaces entirely his: this one for sleeping, another with piles of books and room for piles more, then a place where he could draw and paint away, and make all kinds of shapes with wood and clay and stone, and of course there had to be a space for the chemicals, fireworks and so forth. Imagine the satisfaction in being free to work as you wanted, moving from space to space. All of them, of course, would have to be in Balnahown. Balnahown was the best place on earth.

But today he had to leave Balnahown yet again. That fearsome distance, that awful prison. Two years running it nearly killed him. Beautifully situated, the prospectus had said that time three years ago and he only eleven, this head house of the order, beautifully situated, amid lakes and mountains. Tubbernagur. God, how he hated it!

He knew, he knew: no secondary day school suitable in the environs of Balnahown. He knew his parents had thought a lot about it all; that they had talked with other parents in that part of the county who, with endless care, contrived the wherewithal to get their children educated, the teachers in Moygrane, in Cloonard, in Kyridyne, the doctor and his wife in the village of Tully, even the doctor and his wife—the two of them doctors—in the town of Poulanara. Doctors had it a bit easier, maybe, but all these parents had had to think like his and make decisions about the education of families in the hard times that people were always talking about. That place photographed and described in the prospectus was the winner for boys. Tubbernagur. How he abominated even the name. When he had fallen sick the first term and again the first term in second year, and had to be put into hospital and then sent home to recuperate, his malady was called pneumonia. But it was loneliness. Pining.

Strong feeling about the land. A sort of pulling. A sort of pain. All that land surrounding the house and all going beyond to the whole of Balnahown and further still, that entire western region of bleak hills and bare bog, full of treasures for him. To leave all that was very hard. Sean and Minnie said he'd get over it when he was in with the boys. But he was not in with the boys in the way they meant, not in that rollicking slap-happy way they seemed to be suggesting without using so many words. He still felt alien in that place. He spoke very little of this ever to his parents but misery was plain in his face the day prior to going again to Tubbernagur and they tried saying something rallying. Sean's exhortation about the maths was rallying of another kind. And there was Sean again, yelling this time, from outside the kitchen door.

'For God's sake, Jack, aren't you ready?' He was coming up the stairs now. Jack would have preferred his mother coming to get him on his feet. The feelngs—mixed, uncomfortable—he had in regard to his parents, were always with him. He disliked the word love, avoided it. It was a girl's word. It was a word you'd hear from Una or Minnie or Maggie. Una read her mother's copy of *The Woman's Journal*, the English magazine that came home with the shopping every Saturday. The fact that he was getting away from Una was the only consolation in having to leave home. And there was his father now, outraged, bashing open the bedroom door, and who immediately behind him but Una. Bony, lank hair, sallow skin. There could be only one reason for her coming now and that was to witness with her disgusting kind of enjoyment his unready state and consequent berating. Typical.

The small Ford was by the back door. A late precious acquisition. Purchased after much anxious, often acrimonious interchanges between Sean and Minnie. They had also consulted at length the very few other people in the locality who owned motorcars, if only recently. They had not consulted the O'Gormans at the shop—pipes to pikes, whiskey to pigs' heads. Paddy O'Gorman, undertaker, auctioneer, agent for government free milk and things besides. Doing very well in the meagre region. Although beyond the Sunday suit, of which he divested himself immediately after Mass, he seemed to have hardly a stitch of spare clothes. Wouldn't spend on clothes.

Along the dangerously frozen narrow roads drove Sean, his face tense. Neither he nor his son spoke, Una sat in the the back. Her presence there was quite unnecessary; she followed him around to harass. Jack was convinced. She had been there, watching, when it came to saying goodbye to his mother who gave him a kiss on the side of his head and said, 'Now, now...' in a quick uneven way. He had not responded to the kiss nor did he look at her. His father had the engine running. 'You'd better...' his mother said, again in that up and down way. She gestured towards the yard where puffs of car fumes showed on the grim east blast. Una followed on the heels of his black school shoes, lately polished by Maggie. There was no need at all for Una. None whatever.

The station of Moygrane, where the good land began, was four miles down from the western hills. A small solid cutstone building, a garden with flowers and vegetables in season. Everything very well kept. The Deerings—station master and family—were comparative newcomers, transferred from some other small station in a neighbouring county. In summer their small garden bore profusely. Nothing like it in Balnahown, Minnie said. She was quickly their friend: no-nonsense people, she said; hard workers, clean, and fine gardeners. She gave them homemade butter and buttermilk which they drank and used for making bread; they gave her flowers, fruit, honey. It was remarkable, she said, she had never heard a lie from the Deerings. She did not speak in this adulatory way of the O'Gormans. The Deerings were Protestants.

Mr Deering got Jack's trunk stowed in the luggage van. Sean said 'Thanks, thanks, thanks,' in the way he thanked people not closely known. Excessive, apologetic, with shades of impatience at having to acknowledge obligation. However, he liked Mr. Deering. He liked the few other Protestants still living in the district: the rector and his sister, the middle-aged couples on small farms.

The station platform was fully open to the east wind, more piercing than ever as Jack climbed into the train. Neither he nor his father made a move to shake hands. Sean held his son's shoulder for a second and said, 'Bye now, Jack…and for God's sake mind the maths. God bless now, God bless.' Jack said nothing to either his father or Una. His head was down as he climbed.

Sean did not wait for the last of the train to vanish under the bridge where icicles hung. Enough that the door of the carriage was closed on Jack, who was no longer visible. 'Cold day, cold day,' he called down the platform to Mr Deering, who waved. It was not a day, understood, for lingering: Una and her father got quickly into the car. In the single street of Moygrane the only life visible was a sad donkey tackled to a milk cart, waiting on untrimmed hooves. They parked outside the butcher's.

'Bones,' Minnie had said earlier that morning before they had begun urging Jack to speed up. She was referring to the errand she wished Sean to do for her at the butcher's in Moygrane. He disliked shopping and did it only in extremity. A flood of scathing comments from his wife on his uselessness constituted an extremity: he would carry out the errand. However, Jack being on his mind, he said absently, 'Write it down. I'll give it to him.' The person in question was the butcher whom Sean knew very well and with whom he should not have experienced the slightest difficulty in verbally conveying so elementary a message.

'Specify,' Sean had said to Minnie.

'Lord give me patience, and you a schoolmaster.' She was confining herself, in view of the morning it was, Jack leaving.

Una went past the donkey to the small shop selling newspapers, knicknacks, and ice-cream in summer. She bought, with some of her scarce Christmas money, the only girl's magazine to be had, faded, out of date. Sadie O'Gorman, who was older than her and going away to boarding school in the autumn, sometimes gave her magazines. Sadie had a great knack of obtaining things other girls never seemed to have. In some of the magazines—they came in from England—were stories where brothers called their sisters 'old girl' and helped them to carry things and held doors open for them and visited them in their rooms when they were sick in bed with flu and other unpleasant ailments. These brothers made presents for people in the family, for birthdays and Christmas. They organised games where boys participated with girls and they said 'Jolly good!' and clapped and said 'Well done!' when their sisters won. Una longed for Jack to be such a brother.

The rector, Mr Rydall, charged the wireless batteries for Sean and chatted, telling Sean that he preferred doing things like that and tinkering in his roomy shed, with its accumulated miscellany, to delivering sermons to the mere few, if they turned up at all. Sean hoped Jack wasn't listening. But Jack was. Whenever possible, he accompanied his father on calls to the rectory. Sometimes he even cycled on his own to fetch or deliver the batteries. These visits got him wishing, often fiercely, for that working place of his own, full of things like Mr Rydall's scatter of gadgets and oddments. None of the Protestants was rich, not rich in the way the O'Gormans, for all their hiding of it, surely were, and some of the Catholic business people in the town. But there were things about them that put them on a level different from that of the Catholic population. The rector and his sister had that accent of the BBC announcers. Minnie reacted to it with a prim unnatural voice if ever she spoke with them. That was not often.

Once—it was the first time she had gone to the rectory with Sean, Jack miles and miles away in Tubbernagur—while Una was waiting for the charging process to be finished, she scurried up a tree and slithered madly down again, Mr Rydall's son said, 'Jolly good!' and then he said, 'Well done!' She had never seen him before; most of the year he was at school in England. It was as if he had materialised with that special accent out of one of Sadie O'Gorman's magazines. And then, just at that moment, the rector himself came with her father from the shed carrying the batteries. 'Andrew is home for the long vac,' he said by way of introduction. Andrew looked about fifteen.

'Do come and join us,' Mr Rydall went on, putting the batteries in the boot of the Ford for Sean. 'Elfrida will be brewing tea by now.'

'Ah no, ah no,' Sean said.

'Ah yes, please do. It's Andrew's first day home—a little company, you know.'

And to Una's astonishment, for it was most unlike her father to take tea anywhere outside his own home except on particular long-arranged occasions, they were all going up the wide stone steps of the rectory and into a large room which seemed overflowing with all kinds of objects. Mr Rydall's sister was just setting down a silver kettle on a mat placed upon a table with carved legs. She was wearing a brimless hat, fitting close around her head and ears, yet allowing to be seen a fringe of hair of a peculiar dark orange hue.

'Eustace, you have brought me visitors! How nice! Please, do sit, Mr Normile. And what is this young lady's name? Ah, I like it, so much simpler than mine. Elfrida is very old fashioned, isn't it, Una? Do sit, my dear, won't you?'

Una said nothing and was not too sure where to sit. Many chairs were scattered about.

'Andrew darling, more cups.'

On the table, Una saw, there was also a plate of

small square crustless sandwiches, each showing a pinkish line of filling. Ham, she thought. Ham sandwiches went with the rare visits of the Normile family to the city, where a cousin worked in a café and slid them a few extra on the sly, when they went there for a cup of tea after the shopping. Never were they made at home in Balnahown.

'Milk, Una? Sugar? Andrew, our guests!'

Andrew placed a tiny table just by Una's right hand; he came first to her with the sandwiches. He saw to it that her father equally had a little table handy. It got Sean into a flurry of thanks thanks thanks: constraint was clutching, awkwardness afoot; his cup and saucer seemed a worry, the convenient side table notwithstanding. Tea was not dispensed in this fashion at home. He preferred the home style, no two ways about it. Mr Rydall's anecdote was not getting him to throw back his head, laughing, as it would have done outside.

With surprise, Una found that, after all, the pinkish line was made by raspberry jam. The discovery was disappointing. Sandwiches did not really belong to daily life; at the school, every day, she and her parents ate soda bread slices that Maggie had clamped together with butter. Peetie and the men in the fields ate similar slices, only thicker. She did not think of these as sandwiches. A sandwich was in the nature of excitement, like the visits to the city, and, as far as she expected, it had a tangy, peppery, salty taste. No one had ever given her a jam sandwich until now. This tea, taken with the Rydalls, was quite unlike any taken elsewhere.

At home, the meal called tea was the last one of the day and therefore at a later hour. They all, Maggie included, would sit together around the large kitchen table. When they visited cousins or friends, on agreed occasions, there would be much more to eat than here for the meal called tea: plates of cold meat, breads and scones, biscuits, homemade cakes.

But she was glad of the difference, in spite of the jam filling. There was a quality about the room, about the Rydalls, that held her. The parrot, chained to a perch in the corner, began to squawk; Andrew brought her to see the coloured seeds he fed on. The floor beneath the perch was covered in debris and quite a splatter of droppings. The table, whereon were the silver kettle and remaining sandwiches, also came within the ambit of flying seed husks, of which it now carried something of a display. Elfrida, laughing, flicked at them in a lazy way, not bothering really. Her nails, lacquered red, had grey rims; her skirt was fairly crushed and stained here and there. She smiled a lot and asked many questions and, when Una continued shy in answering, she began to tell her about the part of Africa she had lived in for so long, quite as if Una were a grown-up. Mr Rydall pressed her father to take a nip of whiskey before leaving.

'Ah no, ah no.'

This time Sean was not to be persuaded but Mr Rydall took his own nip in a leisurely way, smiling all the while.

Andrew held the car door open for Una. When she and her father were driving back up the hills, she was longing for Jack to be like Andrew. Jack loved hating. Protestants were nicer. It would be great if they could be Catholics...but they wouldn't be the same then...it was very confusing. She had not liked the grey rim on Miss Rydall's varnished red nails but she had liked very much the way she smiled so often and had spoken to her about Africa as if she were an equal. She hadn't liked either the seed husks and droppings: her mother, while making sure they were well-fed, wouldn't let a cat or dog inside the house. But then, neither did her mother smile as much, nor seem so jolly as Miss Rydall. There was the new car and the petrol; there was the wireless—also new, the only one in their side of Balnahown; there was Christmas, the fortnight's holiday by the long western beach in summer; there were wages for Peetie and sometimes the extra workmen and for Maggie; there were those fearsome college fees for Jack: was it because her mother and father had to worry always about stretching money, was it that that kept them from smiling the way the rector and his sister smiled? The Rydalls couldn't have much money either or else they would have someone to clean after the parrot, and Miss Rydall could buy a new skirt, the door hanging off Mr Rydall's shed could be replaced, he himself wouldn't wear such old clothes with daubs of oil and paint—the priests never appeared like that, like the people working on the land or in the sandpit, or building walls. Yet, the Rydalls had travelled a lot. They all had that BBC accent. Mr Rydall had his own boat waiting by the Shannon. And even though the house was crumbly, there were many things in that room with the parrot and all over the place that looked valuable—or were they just different? Andrew's school, all the way to England, would have to mean a lot of expense.

'Are they rich, Daddy, the Rydalls?'

'Ah-sha, I don't know, childeen. I wouldn't think they are.'

'They have things we haven't.'

'They do, child, they do. They're different. There's

no put-on with them, though.' Then he gave a small laugh. 'Mr Rydall enjoys life,' he said. He added, with another little laugh, 'I enjoy him.'

Had it something to do with their being vicarage people? It was hard to tell. She knew so few other Protestants. There were the Deerings: another kind of Protestant than the Rydalls, different accent—Minnie said the Deerings had an accent you could sit on; she said it approvingly. Cork, it was. They worked very hard. Mrs Deering did her own scrubbing; you could eat off their floors. The Deerings were like the Rydalls only in the way they were always friendly and smiled a lot. Protestants. Una decided she liked the ones she knew.

'Did you notice the hat?' Minnie asked when they told her why they were delayed. 'Hat for tea—one of the marks,' Minnie said, 'the real thing, you know.' She said it in the prim voice, but then she laughed gently.

Sean said, 'Ah-sha, nonsense, nonsense. They're very decent people.'

'That they are. You'd have to like them. True blues I'd call them.' Minnie had her usual voice again, saying that.

Four

The history lessons. Penal Laws. Learning about the English. England, the age-old enemy, who had wreaked appalling cruelty on the Irish people, dispossessed them, denied them their language, the practice of their religion, their culture, their identity, their existence. To hell or Connaught.

That was in the past.

The magazines told you some things about England of the present time. Minnie's niece told some more; she stayed for a holiday having come from working in England. She had worked there first for struggling Jews with a heavy accent; she gave a rendering: '...go fetch the hoil-can unt pliss to go round corner to fetch me some hoil to fry mit the fish.'

She had also worked in London for wealthy Austrian Jews. Bankers, she said, who slept in silk sheets, whose womenfolk let her have the loveliest silk stockings which they rejected at the tiniest sign of a snag in the mesh. So this England of the present was a country where Jews, of different kinds of schooling, wealth and position, employed the Irish who were always poor. A place you got some notion of through the magazines. And from the wireless. Gracie Fields sometimes sang over the wireless songs which Minnie liked—the high-ranging clear ones—or hated—the raucous ones in a Lancashire dialect. (Jack hated the sound of all singing women of any nationality.) England was a place where Henry Hall

had a band, a place from where news was sent across
in that BBC voice. News of the war: Minnie against
the Germans; Jack against the British; Sean said Hitler
was Antichrist. Una was much puzzled by war news.
The foreign names resounded in her head; she kept
hearing them when she went out around the land.

May 1942. In Dublin, Nelson Forterre was a supplier
of vicarious experience. He meant her wider
envisaging of his country, From what he told her of
the England he knew, denigration and pride often
combined in his telling, she could imagine much
more of it. She was getting a wider view, as it were a
feel of the mixing of peoples.

His origins, he said, could be shown to go back to
the Norman conquerors, on his father's side; to
dogged survivors in the life game, some prudent
savers, wild spenders and at least one sagacious
money-maker on his mother's. His mother's side was
the more complicated; several strands went to the
making of it, Polish, German, Scottish, Jewish. Mrs
Forterre was ambivalent about this last one, strong
strand that it was. There were times, depending on
the company, when she dreaded its revealation, was,
indeed, prepared to deny it. Not everyone welcomed
either the German or Jewish colouring of blood. In
his youth, however, her German Jewish grandfather
was considered a suitable spouse for her English
grandmother: most likely his financial position was a
factor of prime importance. Two generations further
on, with an English upbringing, Mrs Forterre herself
seemed thoroughly anglicised, imbued with the
nuances of class-consciousness and all that that
entailed. She kept up with the German connections,
however, and in the family circle showed a

preference for German beer over French wine. A low habit, she said. Her way of sudden self-ridicule was one of her winning aspects, Nelson said. Since the war with Hitler, she did not speak outside family of the German links. As it was, the Forterres were considered well-born. Their inherited way of speech and codes of behaviour which belonged, all contributed to their position in that treacherous territory which considers itself the best society.

Incongruously. Nelson remarked, 'So you see, we do have a few things in common, you and I.'

'What on earth?'

'Well, we —our family—lived in the country, too. Until I was twelve or so. A country very different, granted, from what you describe. A pampered lush land, I suppose. Large properties, well cared for by workmen, tenants often, who lived in cottages on them. My father's aunt had such a property. On its grounds was the vicarage and there we lived. So you see we have country life and a vicarage in common.'

'Great differences, though! Very different country and, from what you tell me, very different vicarage.'

'In any case, our differences are doing fine together so far—true?'

'Seems to be.'

'In fact, by comparison with our wealthy aunt we were the poor relations in the vicarage. The aunt was something of a *grande dame*. We were beholden to her for daily bread. My mother consoled herself by saying that if Great-aunt Gertrude—what a mouthful!—had all the wealth, we looked better. And then she'd laugh because one didn't need much in the way of looks to outdo Aunt G for she was ugly as sin. Amongst ourselves we called the old girl Geegee.' Mrs Forterre said there were more brains in the vicarage family too, although she conceded that the cousins from the manor had put what small brains they had to sensible use in marrying to advantage; she was not at all sure of the commonsense of her own offspring when they came to marrying years.

'But off we go to Balnahown again, Una. It's time,' he urged. 'Come on, more. Much more.'

The January day when Jack left so miserably for Tubbernagur was a day very unlike that one in the summer when she and her father had tea at the parson's house. Branches were layered in frost, the sky menaced; horses, shackled to creamery carts, struggled on the bad roads, in danger of skidding on iced-over potholes.

As they were driving by the field where a path led down to the waterfall, her father did an unusual thing. He stopped the car and said, 'Come on, Una, we'll go down to see the icicles.' It took them quite a while, the path being extremely narrow and twisting with the side of the valley from which thrust out frozen brambles and matted bushes; underfoot, the ground was like pitted metal. There was no sound of falling water as in summer. When they came to the point which gave a sudden view of the waterfall, instead of cascading foam, they saw the whole rock-face hung with icicles of an astonishing variety.

'Now, didn't I tell you?' said Sean who, on the way, had uttered no word beyond 'Come on, girl, hold on there' every now and then as he gave her a saving hand. They stood quite still, just looking, side by side. 'Ah, childeen,' he said after a while. And then, soon, in a different, matter-of-fact voice, 'We'll get our death; we'll go home.' And they did go.

On the range, over the closed turf fire, there was soup.

'What on God's earth kept ye?' Minnie asked.

'The roads are bad,' her husband said.

He did not mention the waterfall. Neither did Una. Instead she showed her mother the magazine. 'Got it with my Christmas money.'

'You're entitled to spend that money the way you want, I suppose, within reason. That magazine is a decent enough sort, not like those comics. Good grammar, that's what I like to see.'

In bed under the cold north eave, that night Una saw. Herself and Jack. A few times, true, they had been...no, almost been, friends. Brittle friends. But some raging thing had always crashed in to destroy.

There was so much going on all the time. You wanted to know about it. But the grown-ups always wanted to shut you out.

Information was very important, that was plain. News, telling things. And laughing. There were so many kinds of laughing. Everywhere people could be heard saying, 'C'm'ere till I tell you.' Women put their shawled heads together as they told; their shawls often slipped back with the jerking of their telling and you could see their faces flash with that particular grown-up laugh that was the sound of secrets. Their faces could look envious as they laughed; they could look even sorrowful in their laughing.

In the schoolroom during the lunch interval, her mother and the assistant teacher, sitting at a small side table, imparted information to each other which was different from what they gave to their classes. Una was not encouraged to listen and Minnie enjoined her to hurry up with her bread and butter, which she ate mostly standing at the edge of the large table whereon were teachers' books and the brass handbell.

'Hurry up, Una, run out to play with the rest. You'll have no time left if you don't hurry.'

Nor did Maggie encourage listening either while, with wild spurts of laughter, she saw to food for Peetie in the kitchen, passing on her latest story and extracting from him another.

'Una, will you get a *gwaal* o' turf.'

'Una, there's that strayin' hen squawkin' again, go an' see if she's layin' in the hedge.'

Nevertheless, Una did manage to hear fragments that tantalised.

Jack put much importance on information. He read whatever he could find and was given to indicating his extra knowledge to his sister in ways that confounded and mortified her, asking her questions about things he knew she knew nothing of. In bed, he read until three or four in the morning.

'Jack, put out that candle. At once. D'you hear.'

But beyond admonishing him thus, they themselves three-quarters asleep in the small hours, Sean and Minnie did not interfere with, nor query his reading. Quite the contrary were they, in regard to Una.

'Jack's a reader,' they said with satisfaction to people.

Apart from what was to be had at home, he got his material wherever possible. There was the travelling library, coming once a month—mostly rubbish, he said, but nonetheless to be availed of; there was Father Twomey at Tubbernagur who gave him French books—a liberal, Jack described him, the one instructor in that place for whom he had affection; in some people's houses you might find the odd interesting book; the uncle in Chicago sent stuff—a lot of that Minnie and Sean wanted to burn; the few particular friends would exchange with you, especially Thady Keane.

Jack gave Una a list of selected words and told her to look them up in the dictionary. He elaborated on the clipped dictionary explanations and sniggered. She disliked his face intensely with that snigger on it. She was, however, having her store of information increased. She saw the dictionary for the first time as other than part of the duller things like the piles of copybooks her parents hauled home for correcting. She resolved to explore it. Doing so, she began to have inklings of some of the reasons for so many heads together, whisperings, sudden mad laughing, knowing looks and silences of a certain kind at her approach. The whisperings would not be in the language of the dictionary but you got some idea of what was going on. Yet there was a great deal of further information she could not come by at home. Boys got it more easily; they could move around more, were not constricted by the same rules that held her in. Being a girl was unfortunate. Unfair. She went down the glen in Balnahown to read the magazines from the uncle in Chicago with their bluish photographs.

'Sean, you ought to tell that brother of yours to stop sending them. Who wants such...such *slush*?'

You couldn't say to your mother that you had a savage appetite for them. Because of some sudden domestic distraction which took her out of the kitchen, Minnie had been held up in the burning of them. They disappeared, anyway, and were aparently forgotten. Meanwhile, they were in one of Jack's many secret places, eventually tracked down by Una. She had her own hidey-holes. The one in the glen was a rocky cavity with a tangle of brambles over the mouth, quite away from Jack's dugout. If you wore old leather gloves, you could manage the briars. There she kept the latest, unacceptable reading store. She herself never had enough to read, getting through any new school reader in a few days and keeping continually on the watch for fresh matter. Besides the Normile uncle in Chicago, there were relatives of other people in Balnahown who occasionally sent newspapers and periodicals—from America, England and, a very odd time, from Australia. Things in them against the sixth commandment, Minnie said, trash. She was on perpetual guard against anything offending that pervasive commandment. The sight of things against it stirred up the strangely wild laughing in some people. Una had seen them looking, had heard them laughing. Horror, terror, lunacy had to do with that commandment. Minnie unrelentingly sought to shield her daughter.

When the Normile hens were running out of eggs, Minnie bought from Mrs Doyle who had Rhode Island Reds.

'Mrs Doyle is a decent clean woman. When you think of it, all she has to do trying to look after Dinny. She's clean about the eggs—no hen dirt.'

Una was often sent to fetch. More than once, Mrs Doyle was not there and Dinny's father produced a pictorial magazine from his pocket, showed Una the undressed women and laughed the laugh that both upset and gripped her, did disturbing things between your legs. She had never heard Mrs Doyle laugh that way; Mrs Doyle probably didn't know such pictures were being carried around in her husband's pocket. Nevertheless, the material, fascinating and disgusting at the same time—about naked women, gangsters, murdered corpses, drugs, a dark and compelling life—was sometimes to be had in the district. Knowing this, Una wondered about ways of coming by it. You certainly wouldn't ask Dinny Doyle's father. You could be quite sure some people would not have it: the Deerings wouldn't. Nor could you imagine Mr Rydall or his sister with it. Andrew? You would be far too shy to ask him. Protestants were nicer. He held the car door open for you. He would think you...what would he think you? Dirty-minded? Revolting? Sadie O'Gorman knew more about all this than anyone; she knew where to get pictures of killer weapons, injecting needles, prisons, night clubs, what the priest called immodest women.

The women in the bluish pictures from Chicago had thin eyebrows and very defined lips, Una studied them seriously. Film stars. Advertisements. Articles. Much was made of what was called allure, sex appeal, glamour. Splendid eyes were emphasised, unblemished skin. Grooming was a word frequently used. Una had always thought it meant getting horses ready for the annual races when the tide was out on the long beach in Ballybunion. In terms of this further meaning, it had to do with detailed routines to maintain—so you were told—skin in seductive softness, eyes of inescapable magnetism, hair sheening as a raven's wing or scintillating as sun-sparkle. The preferred wear for these women seemed to be satin, silk, velvet, fur, kid shoes of delicate fashioning with unbelievably high heels. Una took stock of herself in the light of these requirements for females in places far removed from Balnahown. Her knees and elbows were permanently scarred from tomboy accidents, her legs were goosefleshed; as to shoes, she had always liked best going barefoot from April to October; the only footwear she had was what was considered most resistant to stony winter roads, or laced-up flat summer canvas. Her eyes did not see very far any more—from beside Maggie, she had not been able to see the spectacle of Jack approaching through the well-field with the wrecked boat he'd made pulled up like a knickers, Maggie said, around his waist. The glasses, when she got them, were a another target for Jack's mockery.

'Bad enough to be a parasite, to have a rotten spying telltale nature, without looking more of an eejit than ever with that bicycle on your nose.'

No one in the pictures she examined so minutely wore glasses. A clever American woman was quoted as saying, 'Men seldom make passes at girls who wear glasses.' She was never likely to look like these women. Sadie O'Gorman was pretty, even if the meanness of the O'Gormans didn't let her have many clothes. It was unfair that she was so pretty. But Una resolved never to speak her frustration. Jack would glory in it. Her mother would recommend her to an acceeptance of God's will and say beauty is only skin deep, be thankful for any gifts you have, lucky not to be born like Dinny Doyle. Her father would deny any physical flaws with, 'Ah sure, you're a great childeen.' But she did not feel she was a child any longer. Precocious. She had seen that explained in the dictionary. She thought she was probably precocious. What use was it to be that? The tears were bitter and made her hideous in the small mirror she had begun to carry around with her. Then she thought what often she thought: it didn't matter one bit what a person looked like going about the bogs, hills and glens. In this she rejoiced. Old clothes, bare feet caked in mud, hair tangled from the wind, smell of the bog, cows, new-mown hay, woodbine—all these were what she was happiest with, a happiness sometimes so strong that it was another kind of hurt in the chest.

But undeniably, too, there were pulls to things quite opposite, things outside and away; there was the pull of an ever-sharp curiosity that sought to cut into all the unknown territories beyond.

The larks had not stopped since dawn. She had got up then to see the sky from her bedroom window and thought of going to the high moor. But she had not done so. She would go there now.

Five

May–June 1942

As to the German cousins, Nelson told Una, there had been much anxiety. There were rumours. Stories of discovered identities, regarding Jews. Could the cousins possibly conceal the truth, miraculously survive?

His mother did hear that a couple of them had been coerced into the army. That is to say, they couldn't dare object: to do so was to become a focus of brutal inquiry. As it was, it didn't bear thinking on, Mrs Forterre said, their being made to fight the British. Further, she agonised as to whether they had been subjected to nude scrutiny and if the fact of their circumcision accounted now for the absence of all communication from them since their enforced enlistment. Immolation was the word. You dared not ask anything of this in letters. But you could not help wondering were they already dead.

Before the war, Nelson had spent time with them all. Photos showed him variously, with this one and that in Bavaria in winter, in the Harz Mountains in summer. In Switzerland, he had mountaineered and sailed with other different connections; they had chalets or lakeside houses there.

When he was nineteen, he had taken his bicycle to Poland and Russia to experience contrasting levels of existence. His parents had not wanted him to go but in the end they had agreed. He had been proving difficult to adapt to desirable modes of livelihood: a look at the actualities over there might help him out of his flimsy thinking, his revolutionary misguidedness. On his return, his father had died suddenly.

The vaunted far-stretching lineage and accompanying manifestations of class seemed, from Nelson's youth, of limited practical value to his parents. In reality they were on the edge of things: money was called for to keep up required appurtenances, apparel, hospitality, servants, and so on. The truth was, Nelson's father, the Reverend Paul Forterre, had no head for finances and had, early in his marriage, lost not only a legacy in his own right but one of his wife's as well in ill-advised speculation. His stipend as a clergyman was barely sufficient to keep things going. Amiable, easygoing, quite without ambition, and much liked by his flock—this was how his son described him to Una. Should any wealthy connection bestow any further benisons on the family, these were joyfully welcomed. Their impecuniosity certainly irked the Forterres; it was often humiliating, but amongst themselves they had their times of making fun of it, while always regarding themselves as top drawer.

Sunday afternoons, Una felt, could sometimes drag. After Mass, the pivotal event of the household was the midday meal, always called the dinner. On Friday night Minnie decided what would be eaten as she made out her list for the Saturday shopping in Poulanara. She cooked it with her best attention to tastiness and thrift—the leftovers could be spun out for a day or two into the week. Having cooked it, she ate it only in small measure, as did Una. Maggie ate with greater zest and Sean brought to its consumption an absorbed single-minded purpose, as did

Jack when he was home from Tubbernagur. Conversation was not a feature of the meal. Sean had no small talk and Jack, on his very first holidays from the college, said with decision that eating times were for eating not talking; he had kept to that. The few remarks exchanged among the women usually had to do with features of the food, domestic details, or of the neighbours at Mass that morning. Portions were put aside for Peetie, who would eat on his own after milking time in the evening. This was his preferred way.

Once the meal was cleared away, unless rain was teeming down, Sean, mostly, changed into his oldest battered clothes and took off over the hills and moors after whatever game was in season. Maggie went to see her people in Cloonard. Once Una had gone with her in the donkey cart. She had not liked the house. The corner by the hearth exuded gloom; there Maggie's father brooded behind a walrus moustache. On Sunday afternoon it was Minnie's custom to sit quietly, catching up on some occupation she got no time for during her week of teaching. Jack went to one of his many pursuits which were totally exclusive of Una.

Ever since word of the recently acquired wireless had gone around, there were sometimes Sundays when the afternoon emptiness filled up and Sean didn't make away so fast to the far reaches because some match of importance was to be broadcast. A number of locals—men and older boys—turned up to listen to the renowned sports commentator. It was taken for granted that they could come like this without any previous reference to the people of the house. Relatives, and others who best knew Sean Normile, would be the first into the kitchen, still wearing their Sunday clothes. As they came through the back door, they said, 'God bless all here.' Sean replied, 'And you too.' If she were there, Minnie would say it with him but in a way very slightly patronising: it was, after all, her kitchen, her convenience being used and then too, of course, she had been a woman of the town, where greetings went differently. But on these occasions, Minnie mostly gathered herself off, as she put it, meaning she went to another room and stayed there, doing her usual Sunday afternoon catching up. Sports interested her not at all. The men or boys who didn't know the Normiles so well remained at first around the yard or outhouses, trying to handle their shyness. They'd exhange a word or so with Peetie and, a few steps at a time, gradually push nearer the kitchen door. When the match finished, all who had come would move out again, mostly without a word to the man in whose house they had been—sitting or standing, according to their luck or feeling of ease in the place. The absence of address on their part arose again from shyness, awkwardness. A few did say, 'So long, Sean' or 'Day to you now, Master,' depending on their degree of familiarity. Sean would walk out the door with the last to go, seeing them the traditional piece of the way. With him, it was a very short piece and, since he was not a talker, he said the least possible.

Like Minnie, Una had no interest in sports and the occasional matches and filling up of the Sunday afternoon emptiness meant nothing to her beyond her wondering, a few shaky times, would her small advancing signs of femaleness gain any gratifying recognition were she to weave her way among the crowded males. Once, she did slip through them and, although her eyes were downwards, she sensed something in her father's face that gave her a feeling he knew what she was about. This was a most uncomfortable result and, subsequently, she left the house by the front door on those match Sundays. Almost always, anyway, she preferred to be away wandering about the land on Sunday afternoons.

This Sunday, she would go to Daly's Hill and bring back the stone. She had found it buried in the fine sand which made the hill. It was really only half a hill now since the Daly's, once they discovered it, were selling the yellowish-grey sand hand over fist. Naturally enough, for they badly needed the cash. The stone was unlike any she had ever seen. Too big for her to lift. It was pink and glazed; in parts, the glaze was just a thin cover over a multiplicity of small variegated pebbles all held tightly together. An extraordinary thing, a splendid stone, and she had remained there in the sandpit, rubbing it free of sand, absorbed in its remarkable revelations when her school companions, tired of her exclamations, had gone on without her.

'You're mad, Una, only an old stone.'

She caught up with them, having hidden it. The path they took over the bog from Daly's Hill was their shortcut in fine weather.

At home, in the course of tea, she told of the stone. Had Jack been there, she might have restrained her enthusiasm but Jack was safely out of the way at Tubbernagur. She said she wanted it home.

'Peetie could bring it with the horse and cart.' Peetie was not at the table.

'Ah, childeen,' Sean remonstrated and went on spooning up the stewed apple which was the principal item for tea this evening to go with the soda bread Maggie had baked and the butter Minnie had churned.

'Heaven's sake!' Minnie said. 'Hasn't Peetie the topdress on his mind these days, not to have him distracted going back to Daly's Hill for just a stone.'

'But it's a stone like no one has ever seen before. I'm sure and certain you have never seen a stone like it.'

'What ails you, girl?' Maggie was laughing bits of crumb at the notion. 'A stone!'

'You could carry it in the boot of the car for me, Daddy.'

'Did you think at all,' said Minnie, 'what would the Dalys have to say to us, taking just the stone, mind you, and buying no sand?'

'Daddy?'

Sean's forehead became ridged. 'You know I drive the car out only when I have to.'

'But Daddy, the Dalys wouldn't want that stone; they'd only break it up with a sledgehammer for mending the roads. They wouldn't mind if we took it. I covered it up but still, if we don't get it quick, it could get put into someone's load of sand and I'd lose it, never again to see it.'

'Ah childeen, I've plenty on my mind tonight...'

'You can't have as much as I have,' Minnie cut in, swift and sharp, 'and all the socks I've to mend as well as the copybooks to correct. But 'tis true, Una, leave us alone about that stone of yours. We have enough to think about.'

So Una said no more, knowing the strength of the opposition. None of them would see the matter her way. But she decided to do anything possible to have the stone in spite of all. That had been Friday evening. She could do nothing about it on Saturday for Minnie had already decreed she must go to

Poulanara that day for a haircut. And now, this Sunday afternoon she took one of the old coarse hempen sacks from the few Peetie kept in the shed. She walked with it to Daly's Hill which, today, was deserted. The stone was where she had left it concealed. She manoeuvred it into the sack and, pulling that along the ground, made off to take the shortcut home through the bog. The day was dry.

From the top of what was left of Daly's Hill, she could look down on the marshy acres known as Scagach. It stretched east to become the moorland part of Balnahown. At the furthest point before the land rose again, could be seen the tips of the two chimneys on her own house. The men would still be there listening to the match. The shortcut path would take her past only one dwelling, that of the Whelans—Mick Whelan, his wife Mary Ellen, his brother Fonsie.

The piece of land drained and reclaimed by the brothers showed green against the surrounding brown spongy ground. The shallow Scagaire river, really no more than a stream, bounded the carefully tended garden where the brothers grew small patches of varying crops. They had the name of being tightfisted, keeping out of pubs on fair days. Mick Whelan bought what foodstuffs and other things he decided Mary Ellen should use. Once a year they killed a pig and pickled the meat. There would be no other meat in the house until the next killng. Mary Ellen was rarely seen at the O'Gormans' shop, since the household goods she was permitted were already purchased by 'themselves' as she always called the two men. Sometimes, because the hen and egg money was allowed her, she asked passing school-children to take a few eggs to O'Gorman's for her in the morning and bring in exchange their value in some item when they returned in the evening after school.

The schoolchildren always preferred to the road the shortcut past her house, weather being fair—the Scagaire, narrow though it was, could sometimes flood and become impassable. They would rush down the back half of Daly's Hill and across the Scagach to reach the hedge around Whelan's sunken yard, out of breath and thirsty. They would ask Mary Ellen for a drink of water. She liked their coming and always added 'colourin' to the water, meaning a light clouding of milk—a local token of goodwill—when water was asked for. This she did in spite of the miserly men who would straighten up from their work in the garden to watch venomously until the 'scholars' had gone on their way.

A pale gaunt woman, Mary Ellen; people said she went strange after her only child died in infancy. Minnie sometimes brought homemade butter to her and sometimes rhubarb with a pound of sugar.

'Themselves spend a lot of the day diggin' and diggin' but they won't grow things I'd like. No rhubarb.'

Una, who occasionally went with her mother on visits to chosen neighbours and carried for Minnie the little offerings she liked to bring, would place the bundle of rhubarb on Mary Ellen's table and remain quite quiet in the dim corner by the door. It sometimes worked: sometimes they forgot about her so that one time and another she heard things. She had heard Mary Ellen, with great sorrow in her face, tell Minnie, 'I was too old to have another child.' With simple candour she went on. 'I was old anyway when I married Mick Whelan; it was a miracle I even had the child. The match was made on the strength of the few pounds my father left me.' In her face you could see her profound regret that such a tie was ever put on her.

'There now, Mary Ellen,' Minnie said with feeling and then she said no more as if she was, unusually, lost for words: what was to be said to so dire a predicament? After a few moments, however, she said what she so frequently did when faced with the inexplicable. 'God is good.'

Mary Ellen uttered no blasphemy of rebellion against the deity; incomprehension and great grief were in the bending of her head, in the way she was wiping her cheeks with her hand.

'Themselves,' she began brokenly, 'they don't want me saying it, but it was the damp that killed the child. They get savage with me for going on about the damp but this place of theirs is drownded through and through, what with the boggy ground, the river and the rain.'

As if in a gesture against the bareness, the dankness of her life, she grasped closer to her the short brown shawl she always wore in the house.

'They have the rheumatics but they don't want to let on, they don't want to give me the satisfaction of being proved in the right.'

It was plain she did not think of it as at all her place, this territory where she was living out her stark days. As she continued with complaints about 'their place', she darted looks about her while the rapid words came like a long-dammed flood searching release, yet held in a particular control. Her voice, although fiercely charged, was kept low; it was as if in the longed-for relief of an outburst, she was ever mindful of dangers.

'Themselves can hear the grass growing. The way things turned out, 'tis like I married two men at the same time for the one is always ready to take up where the other leaves off, and sometimes the two together. Bullies. Tyrants.'

'There, there,' Minnie tried unsurely again; it was clear she respected the confidences, feeling deep pity, but was also uncertain as to what the last piece of information signified: could it be something unspeakable? She wanted to comfort, while dreading that no earthly comfort was possible.

Pulling the stone in the sack was proving more difficult than Una had imagined. The sack was old; like the other sacks Peetie kept in the shed, it had served over a long period many uses involving wetting and no attention to drying out, and its weave was half-rotten. Fairly soon a hole got worn as she dragged it along; changing the point of friction only created further holes. She tied the two corners of the mouth together and tried pulling the weight at that end but there, too, as she neared the Whelans' house, yet another hole was spreading. She thought to ask Mary Ellen for help—a few bits of string to tie up the holes might just help to hold the thing together and get her valuable load home. Or, best of all, Mary Ellen might give her a better sack.

She did not see either of the brothers in the fields. Neither had she noticed them on the boreen which led to the back of the house. She hoped they were not inside. She did not like them and believed they would jeer at her stone in the bag and the whole notion of wanting to carry it down to her house.

She left her burden on the path and went through the gap in the hedge commonly used as an entrance to the sunken yard. The kitchen door was open and she gave a little knock on it. There was no sound except the squawk of a hen from within. Then, from where she stood, she noticed Mary Ellen's muddy old boots that she wore to clean out the henhouse but that now, in the strangest way and with Mary Ellen's legs projecting from them, were pointing towards the turf-lined roof. Moving further in, Una could see Mary Ellen stretched on the hard mud floor. Her face was a featureless mash, her head gaped open near the wall where whitewash was spattered red. A hen stood on her stomach, pecking at something on her apron. There was a spade lying on the floor, its edge in a splodge of thickening blood, its handle towards the hearth, over which a hanging pot was quietly steaming.

Minnie, having the kitchen to herself again once the men had all gone, had been standing at the range, waiting for the kettle to boil, She reached sideways for the arm of Sean's big sugawn-bottomed chair and felt her way into it, staring all the while at Una. The tops of her cheeks had become suddenly very flushed. 'Lord save us!' was all she could manage.

It was Maggie who informed the gardai. It was she, having returned from the visit to her people and feeding the Normiles' hens in the warm April evening, who was the first to see Una's shivering return. Sean was still out on the mountain, having gone there when the match was finished and all the listeners had departed.

Minnie repeated 'Lord save us all!' many times and then she said a number of other things in a distracted way, turning between Maggie and Una. 'Maggie, you'd better cycle to the barracks this minute. There's no knowing when Daddy will be back. I'd rather we didn't have to be mixed in a thing like this at all—it's terrible that Una was the one to come across it. Daddy won't like it. What'll people think? We told you not to be bothering with that stone—God save us! You're very disobedient. I know it wouldn't bring Mary Ellen back but I'd rather it was someone else found her and it's awful that Una was the one. In God's name, it'll have to be reported straight away.'

In the ensuing days rumour followed upon rumour. For some time no trace of the two men was to be had. Then Mick Whelan was found, arraigned, and awaited trial. His brother Fonsie continued missing in spite of all searches. There were remote streches where a man could hide, but what about food?

Six

The weather held well. Several Saturdays running Una and Nelson had cycled up to the hills. Heather all about, if not yet in bloom. Larks sang. Here were bog asphodel, orchids, all the other moorland flowers she knew so well. Wild smells on the breeze. It was like Balnahown. Quite unlike the packed air in the digs where the odours of cooking had nowhere to go except to penetrate the bedrooms, cling to the landing and coats on the rack in the hallway. Quite unlike the heavy pall in the office—three smokers, the boss's beery breath after lunch, Kitty's repairing nail varnish, the decaying scales of the poor eczema-plagued wretch, in the telephone grooves, on the documents she retrieved after his signature, necessary since he was her senior. Longing for mountain air since leaving Balnahown had been answered, up to this, in the earlier spring outings with her friends from *Craobh an Dóchais*. It was now summer and Nelson Forterre was with her. These were outings of a different nature altogether.

'You might like to come to Penn Reades's next Friday evening?'

'Who is Penn Reade?'

'A friend.'

'On Fridays I like to go to the *Craobh*, you know.'

'Ah...I see. What is this cr...cr...crave—is that how you say it?' The word came oddly from him.

'You could call it a club. And no, that is not how

63

you say it but no matter.'

'Couldn't you go another evening?'

Since that day in the Pine Forest with the inter-university group, when they had first met, she had missed several evenings at the *Craobh*. There was the art class she had taken up once a week. Then there had been what Nelson called the 'first nights'. There had been two of those, one at the Gate, one at the Abbey. He got free tickets because of the reviews he sent off to London. There had been the evening of the curry dinner in a place run by his Indian friend who was doing law in Trinity.

'Very reasonable,' Nelson had said. 'I don't know how it's worth his while.'

The Indian friend had given them a warm welcome. Only a few other people were eating. Nelson had asked for half-portions.

'They will be plenty,' he said to Una, in a mixture of reassurance and apology, when the friend had gone to see to what he had ordered. Curried food was new to her, as was the expression half-portion. These days she had a hefty appetite, different from the finicky days of childhood. An appetite like it was surely coarse, deplorable, but there it was, leaving her now secretly threatened by the thought of a half-portion. He must have felt her thinking it. She knew the matter of cost had always to be remembered. She knew, too, she was missing more evenings from the *Craobh* than she felt altogether easy about. She missed yet another one when she cycled with him to the white rabbit farm on which he was to write an article. The press photographer had already been there and gone.

She began to feel traitorous about the *Craobh*. If he

knew Irish she was sure they would have gone there together. But he did not. It was quite unlikely that he would have either time or inclination to learn it. But he was a person such as she had not met before. Already she seemed to be making him a first concern. When she met the friends in the street, they spoke together in Irish as always. They asked her why she had not been coming so often.

'There were...things,' she replied vaguely.

They looked at her and said they knew, they could guess. Why didn't she bring him too?

'He doesn't know any.'

'Sure we could teach him, couldn't we?'

'Not this one, I think. He is very...English—no ear at all for it. He's not one to go down to Dingle nor over to Connemara nor up to Gweedore to saturate himself in *blas*.'

'Aye-yeh,' they said. 'Would you believe it? And you that were the fierce Irishwoman!'

She made no smart answer. She was feeling guilty. She said she would come the next Friday.

'Couldn't you?' Nelson queried again, 'Go another night instead—to the...whatever you call it, I mean?'

'Say it,' she said. He said it his way. She corrected. It still came out his way.

'I'd be no good at it, I imagine. Will you, will you come to the Reades'?'

'What is this Penn Reade?'

'*What* is he? A-ah...he's a lot of things, I suppose. He's independent-minded for one. I've had a great many battles with him. Keep having them. Keep trying to work things out. In fact, it was he who recommended that I do the course in Trinity. I don't think I'd have done it otherwise. So, if you like, we probably would not have met but for him—another way of seeing it.'

'You like him?'

'I find a good deal to like in the way he approaches things.'

A hare suddenly flashed past. A curlew called.

'Will you come, Una? To the circle?'

'Circle?'

'Oh, we just call it that—the Friday circle. Just a way to describe the gathering.'

'Tell me more about it, about him.'

'Well…what shall I say…I suppose in Ireland he is seen as English despite his claim—legitimate claim, too—to nothing but Celtic ancestry. But he is seen as English for various reasons—born in England, lived there half of his life, has an English accent. He meets with a good deal of castigation here. Different grounds for it—some of his views. He is against violence, against whatever separates people, races…'

She broke in. 'But surely people don't fault him for that?'

'Well…he is often called an armchair reformer— you see, he will not participate politically. Battles in another way. Then, to be identified with the English can still be…unfortunate for one, here. I've lived here myself a number of years now and only seldom have I experienced vestiges of hostility regarding my origins. But Penn Reade is a controversial entity. To some, he is a man of courage, even heroic, in breaking through frontiers of thinking, in a willingness to explore patterns of coexistence. Broadly put, he holds that the real battles are those with ourselves. Some abhor his insistence on honest self-scrutiny, finding it preferable to sneer at him, as I just said, and call him an armchair reformer. From my time here in Ireland, it seems to me that the wounds of the struggle for Independence are still sometimes hardly skinned over—not to be wondered at, that. But it strikes me that to be a hero here means you drew someone's blood or someone drew your blood. Penn Reade undertakes many struggles with people, for people, but they are the struggles of trying to work out close relationships. He has the belief that there, at those individual levels—the human being at issue with his fragmented self, selves, or person to person—love and hate are in primary but all-important conflict, the roots of violence. At those levels, he attempts to have matters resolved. I say attempts. It is there he focuses energy. His own daughter Madeline is often at odds with him. I suppose I find his open-minded approach more satisfactory than the imposition of dogma and edicts.'

They were both silent for a while. A quiet wind came down the mountain. After a time he asked once again, but lightly, 'So what do you think, Una? Might you feel like coming?'

'You see I really did promise to go to the *Craobh* on Friday…you see I missed nights…'

'Look, what if I said I'll come with you there, to the *Craobh*, on say Tuesday instead?'

'What? You?'

'Yes, I'm curious about this…club, crave or however you say it.'

'They won't talk English.'

'I'm no talker anyway.'

'It's a place where they talk Irish only.'

'All right. Suits me; that's fine. I'll listen. I can go

away again if they don't like me there.'

He had little time: why was he proposing to use some of it in such an activity? Yet she said, 'Well...yes...I suppose we could try, just this once. You are going only out of curiosity and...'

He cut in, 'What's wrong with curiosity? A valuable commodity, curiosity. Makes for advancement. You are always saying you are curious about this that and the other—besides, don't forget my journalistic training: journalists ought to be curious.'

'...and you have no intention of learning the language. Your going will be a sort of intrusion. But...all right. I'll go to Penn Reade's...some time ...instead.'

'Fine. So now.' He was rummaging in the old army canvas bag he carried with him a lot of the time. 'I've brought a bite to eat, a currant loaf—have some.'

There was never anything exciting to eat on outings to the hills. Question of money.

'I should have brought sugar buns.'

'Oh no, not those. This loaf at least does not ooze sugar.'

'And there's plenty dandelion to hand—go on, have some. All free.'

'You should get Mrs Breen to give you sandwiches. I get Commons when I go back to Trinity—proper dinner. Will you?'

Mrs Breen did not supply meals outside the usual routine. After the outings Una had been hungry but they were worth it—up to now, anyway. If they continued, she would see about the sandwiches. For some reason, she had shied away from asking. Her piece of currant loaf—it was really just yeast bread with a few currants thrown in—went down very quickly.

The moss was soft.

Quite some time later, Nelson said, 'Balnahown?'

Seven

Another Sunday late afternoon. No match on the wireless today.

There had been high words between Sean and Minnie, a not infrequent occurrence. Una could hear the sounds of acrimony as she was approaching from the fields, although there was silence when she came in. Sounds of disagreement between them always distressed her. She longed for parents in total harmony as she longed for Jack to be the the sort of brother she read about in those English magazine school stories.

Her father was taking down his gun from the top of the dresser where he always kept it with the box of cartridges, out of general reach. He was six feet and some inches. Minnie was about ten inches shorter and, from that height, ruled. Going out on the mountains with the gun and dog, ostensibly to shoot game in season, served probably much of the time to ease a bothered state, to walk off some of the pressure of worries that were forever mounting inside him. Trying to talk anything out with Minnie never relieved matters and usually ended in the added stress of high words and defeat: her words were always the higher as was her will to win.

He had not returned when twilight was thickening; often it could be dark before he got home. It had been raining over an hour now.

'We'll just go on with the tea, Maggie.'

It was not Minnie's custom to wait for Sean at

these times.

A knocking sounded on the back porch.

'I'll go,' Maggie said. A forward girl and strongly built, she was nevertheless pushed back by the figure advancing into the kitchen. He was almost as tall as Sean. His clothes were caked in mud and to be seen in his hair were bits of twig and withered grass; water dripped from his trouser ends and boots; there was a frightening wildness in his eyes. He stood there, Fonsie Whelan, saying nothing, not looking at anyone but staring around above their heads. The tops of Minnie's cheeks got that bright flush that ran to them in times of sudden strong feeling. She said, in a voice attempting to be level, 'We have just made tea, Fonsie—would you like a cup?'

He did not answer and it was to be seen he had an open penknife in his hand. This he now flung up at the low wooden ceiling where it stuck amid the browning oblongs of bacon. From his height, he reached easily upwards and pulled it out again, only to repeat his previous throw. He seemed set to keep up indefinitely this pull and throw, the women and Una watching helplessly.

It was Sean's return, the gun under his arm, which broke into the rhythm. Before now, Una had not thought about her father's shape although she had been glad he was tall and bony, not butty and lardy like Sadie O'Gorman's father. Neither had she thought of him as brave the way men in stories were brave because, in the arguments with her mother, he was always defeated, afterwards sulking or going out on the hills. If ever she asked whether she was allowed to do one thing or another, he almost always referred her to her mother. 'Be said by your mother.'

However now, she saw his height was important

and more important again was the way he behaved. With the gun he did nothing beyond shift its weight. He never carried the gun loaded near his home; she believed he would never point it at a person, so strongly did he emphasise to Jack, herself and anyone else who might be there, the dangers of pointing even an unloaded gun at anyone, the absolute laws governing its proper use for game hunting only, the inflexible rule of never standing in front of the barrel and so on. He would impress these things in his anxious furrowed way, as he cleaned it in a corner of the kitchen.

On his coming in now, he had given the customary greeting, 'God bless all here', and then he said quietly, 'Good evening to you, Fonsie. Maybe you'd lend me your knife to help with a dodgy cartridge that's jammed here—an empty one of course.'

Minnie, for once, did not in any way put herself forward. She was leaning over the table, holding the edge of it. As Sean stood there, his eyes were above the level of Fonsie Whelan who, without any further movement, handed him the knife. Sean clicked open the gun and tinkered a few seconds so that there was no doubt what he was doing.

'I'd say Fonsie could do with a mug of tea and maybe there's a bit of stew from dinnertime. Sit there now, Fonsie.'

In the ordinary way of things, with Minnie present, Sean would never utter anything like a suggestion or directive in the handling of kitchen matters.

The women stirred; Minnie remained subdued, allowing Sean a clear lead. But there began a renewal of usual mealtime sounds, the moving of tableware, the shifting of utensils on the range, the tending to its fire. Relief was evident in these noises and in the way they began to speak in rapid short sentences.

'Get more milk Maggie, will you?'

'Yes, missis, I'll start on the last can.'

'Una, there's not enough turf.'

'I'll bring more, Mam.'

All was agreement and cooperation.

Una wrote about it to Jack. Several times she had written to him since he had first gone to Tubbernagur. Not once had he answered. When he came home he ridiculed the letters. They sounded, he said, like letters you could imagine out of those namby-pamby magazines of hers that gave her all the wrong ideas about boarding school, which was nothing like what she seemed to think. This time he could not say she was just copying English magazines; this time he might write back. But he grudged her everything, maybe even so horrible an experience: nothing like the Whelan thing had ever happened to him. She wrote, in any case.

She told him how Fonsie Whelan had swallowed down the plate of stew like a hungry dog. He hadn't said a single word all the time. When he was finished, he just got up and rushed out the door into the dark yard. He hadn't got the knife back from their father, who seemed to have forgotten to return it and no one noticed what he'd done with it for they were all watching the man gulping down the food even if they were pretending not to. Their father had not followed him out in the usual way to go a piece of the road with a caller. 'Isn't it as well we don't know anything more about him—which way he took or whatever? If they come asking, all any of us has to say is that he came and went and we don't know anything more. That's the truth now.' This was what Sean said in the kitchen. 'Better not get mixed up in that sort of a thing. There's no knowing the ins and the outs of it.' Minnie did not disagree.

Jack ignored the letter as far as writing to Una was concerned. But in his weekly compulsory supervised missive to his parents, he indirectly alluded to it, saying it looked as if there were queer goings-on in Balnahown. He said he'd got his maths grade in the monthly test and that ought to please them

What had happened was hideous. Una knew it. Her being the first to come upon the hideous thing gave her a special place. An importance. It was a horrible kind of importance but even so he would not indulge her with one pesonal word about it.

The murder case dragged on. As it happened, Fonsie Whelan was taken into custody soon after that Sunday evening. It would seem he had lost whatever cunning or luck had kept him at large thus far. The gardai on the watch had found him injured and exhausted in a ditch near the scene of the crime. A murderer always returns there, Maggie said. Subsequently, he was put into the county asylum.

'That's what he was after,' Minnie said. 'Cunning enough. That's why he came here acting the lunatic. Better the asylum than the rope—that's what was behind all that caper!'

Beyond saying, 'Ah-sha,' Sean said nothing at all and would not be drawn into any talk about the whole business. The case dragged on for so long that people, in a way, lost interest; in another way, it became everyone's story, with as many twists as there were tellers of it.

There were other dark instances. Having so closely witnessed one, Una, disturbed and altered by it in ways only little understood by herself and those nearest to her, heard bit by bit of further violences.

Ever since she had begun, when about six or seven, to go off by herself all through the Normile land, she would remain for quite long periods standing, sitting or lying on one or other of the high points, gazing on and delighting—as her father delighted, as did Jack who would never acknowledge it—in the ever-varying aspects wrought by season, light and shade on the spreading scene all about her which went north over the Shannon and into Clare as far as Slieve Callan. She saw it with a difference now.

Loving the panorama, as always, to a degree sometimes as sharp as pain, she knew now that, here about her—where the cuckoo call, soft, elusive, spoke of summer's arrival, where the lark, exulting on high, confirmed it—crazed things could happen. Here, in many of the homes all about, was much poverty. This she had always known: she went to school each day with the boys and girls making up the classes her parents taught. She knew she was lucky by virtue of her parents' salaries not to be living in the extremes of deprivation she often saw when she went with her companions to their homes. But there were other things of which she now became more aware, things which in part she had known something of without really giving them thought. In any direction around her, in remote small holdings reached only by donkey tracks, or paths and rudimentary stiles, there were to be found living in one small, nigh-derelict, house, combinations of middle-aged or elderly people confined to one another. They could be spinsters and bachelors—sisters and brothers; a barren wife with her bitter husband, her triumphant if demoted mother-in-law; baulked and ageing sons, waiting for a tenacious old father to die. From things she heard with ears newly attuned since the Whelan murder, she understood without so many words that the peevishness and spite in human nature, suppurating with the infections of close proximity and inescapable presences, could aggravate to danger, brutality, lunacy, bloodshed. A person going along the tracks and paths by these houses might sometimes hear vicious wrangling, women's voices in a frenzy, the maniacal howling of men, the striking of flesh. A man had brought in his hayknife from the haggart to slit the barren mattress in two; his wife's half he threw on the dungheap. Another had poured paraffin over, and set fire to, his brother's donkey. The 'county asylum' were two words to be heard very often when people talked.

Una thought a number of times of the stone, abandoned that day in the old sack of holes above the Whelan's sunken yard. She wanted it but did not want to return to the place. However much they urged her, she refused since the horrific event to take the shortcut past the Whelan deserted house, with her school companions who themselves were morbidly eager to do so.

'Daddy, I'd like the stone, after all.'

'Ah childeen, are you going to start on that again?'

'Ah don't, Una.' Minnie was uncharacteristically mild.

'But Mam, I *would* like it—only I don't want to go there, not by myself.'

Then, in an unprecedented way, Peetie was instructed to take the cart to O'Gorman's for some provisions which would normally have been bought at Neary's General Grocery & Hardware in

Poulanara.

'The two of ye go with Peetie,' Minnie said to Maggie and Una. 'When you're coming back,' she said to Peetie, 'you could go up the boreen to Whelans' place, and see,' she turned to Una, 'if you can find that stone, in God's name—and let me hear no more about it.'

Una did find it, almost in the exact spot where she had deposited it in the rotting sack. She did not look at the Whelans' house but urged Peetie and Maggie to put the stone quickly in the cart and go.

'We'd better,' Maggie said, 'it's not a good place to be.' She made the sign of the cross.

A recent flood had swept away a piece of the river bank near where stood the horse and cart and Una stopped to look at the altered contour, although a moment before not wanting to linger. What she was seeing was another stone left bare in the bank after the flood. It was about the same size as the one she had but otherwise it was dissimilar, being almost black and riddled with a multiplicity of openings which looked like the mouths of little passages.

'Peetie, please get it for me.'

'Tis a mania for stones you have,' Maggie said, 'but get it for her anyway, Peetie, and we'll be making off, in God's name.'

When they got home Una asked them to put the two stones in the patch of garden she had made for herself alone at the back of the house.

'Aren't you afraid they'll bring you bad luck?' Maggie asked.

'Maybe I am,' Una was thinking but she said, 'They'll be good luck. They come from a time away back—nothing to do with all that...Anyway, they are lovely stones.'

'Jesus!' Maggie let out, 'you're a quare one!'

She left Una to herself and went into the house to take up the chores from which she had been given temporary and unexpected reprieve.

Peetie stood by a while longer, saying nothing, just looking at Una and then the stones, smiling the while. Peetie did not remember his mother. There was some far out blood link between her family, Sean had said, and the Normiles. Maybe, Una was imagining, Peetie understood in some way what she herself felt about the stones.

'Peetie, will you hurry up with untackling the horse and bring some turnips from the pit.' Minnie's voice indicated that the day's indulgence was over. 'Una, I have a job for you in here.'

Eight

June-July 1942

Going up the stairs to *Craobh an Dóchais*, Una and Nelson could hear a woman's voice loudly railing in English.

'I thought you said no English...'

'Yes, I did, and it's true. I have never heard anything like this here before.'

The woman was not inveighing against the small group of young people collected there, standing or sitting variously around the room. They seemed at a loss before her. The lousers supposed to be running the country were her target. She had come to them here at the *Craobh*, she said, because, as earnest young people working for fair play in the country, they would surely put her case strongly to the government, those bastards. Since his breakdown, not a penny had Proinsias nor the child and herself been allowed in the line of help from that crowd of gets. And all Proinsias had done, a genius like him, for the language, the books he had written, and all the translations he had done for them. And now left stretched out and rotting there, not able to do a stroke for himself.

She had drink taken, yet was not so drunk that she could not stand squarely and use her etiolated hands emphatically. She looked stained and draggled, her hair trailing limply out of an ineffectual bun. A fine forehead, large eyes, a face that registered hard times. The girl of about seven with similar eyes and forehead and who stayed quite quietly beside her, seemed to take all the agitation as a matter of course.

Una and Nelson remained near the door. Some of the members had smiled at her knowingly as the two of them entered—So that's the fellow himself, said the smiles. An older man, one of the founding members, now came in and spoke in Irish to the woman. She said, 'Sure you know I don't speak the lingo. And isn't that the funny thing now that Proinsias chose me, with no Irish and small schooling, and all the Ireeshians with education he could have.' Hoarsely she laughed.

'Mrs de Burca, I think you know we are already working on Proinsias's case. We are doing what we can.'

'I know, I know…I came in to let off steam. I came in for consolation. 'Tis hard all alone. They are nice young people all of them here around me. I'll tell you there's something else I came for and that's maybe the real reason I came in…I'm terrified in the night the way he goes raving. I can't take any more of that by myself. The hospital sent him back, as you know—I was wondering if any of you good people would take turns to come up and stop with me in the night. 'Tis a lot to ask but he's a special creature, a neglected man, a crucified man. 'Tis no wonder he goes raving mad. I do get terrified and so does Gráinne.'

The child's large eyes had a faraway look.

Tubbernagur. There were ten of them, standing about a foot apart, forming the ring. In the middle of the grass, newly green and pushing up over last year's fall of leaves, was Jack's college cap, holding the money from their meagre pocket allowances. The agreement was an equal amount from each and the winner—the first to ejaculate—took the jackpot minus a tip for the umpire. The place was quiet, selected for that reason, no soutaned prefects on the prowl. Through the oak trunks, a shine of lake in the afternoon sun; beyond the lake a flank of mountain. They were looking at neither the lake nor mountain but at the umpire aloft on an upturned water barrel beside Jack's cap. They awaited his signal. 'One, two, three, begin!'

When it was over they buttoned up. A snigger, an uncertain 'Jaysus!', a hurrying mutter, eyes meeting and not, one outright wild laugh and that was from Thady Keane, the winner. They went their ways towards the college buildings, to corridors, books, changing rooms. The lake, the wood, the mountain flank were as before, territories of their own multitudinous diverse climaxes.

'Guilty, aren't you?' Thady turned to Jack.

'Shut up, pagan.'

'Well you are, you're regretting.'

'Yes, regretting giving in to your smart-aleciness and taking part in that damn lakeside caper. Orgy.'

'Call that an orgy?'

'Atheist. No conscience. No fear of sudden death and hellfire.'

'What else would I be? My father with his science, my mother with her archaelogy—no one ever mentioned a glimmer of hell. No ghastly sixth commandment. No Mass.'

'Lucky.'

'All in the mind. The parents said nothing to the brasshats here. Did not reveal the godless truth. Thought they'd spare me the breathings of redemption down my neck.'

'Godless? How easy if you believe it!'

'So you see, to keep them out of my hair here in Tubbernagur, I go along with the rituals. I can get a laugh out of them. I can take a stand if necessary if the time is right—but that will be after here.'

'Ah, the easy conscience—*that* I envy you. Lucky. Accident of birth. How odd the business of birth. Parents—why weren't yours mine? But no, I don't wish that either, not in full, anyway...oh shut up, Keane! You bring out the worst in me.'

It was time for his session with Father Twomey. Extra, but freely given. Ah yes, they loved French, the two of them. Decent bloke, Twomey. Didn't lay on the religious stuff.

Thady Keane later described to Una, the telling clearly pleasing him. 'I don't want to hear,' she said. But she had already heard.

He couldn't stand the town of Poulanara, Jack said. The smells of it! Always stenching water oozing out back drains. A pile of miasmic pelts and nauseating entrails behind the slaughterhouse. On a summer's day, the bluebottles went straight from there to the sugar buns on the counter in the cake shop. He never wanted to go to Poulanara, he said many a time. The idea of wanting him to cycle down the six miles there and then walk back up the long hill, just to buy a pound of tomatoes!

'Well, you can get your hair cut too, it badly needs cutting. The O'Gormans don't ever sell tomatoes as you know well and they're not to be had in Moygrane either. Do it Jack, do your share. You're so seldom asked.' That wasn't the truth, anyway, he was often asked.

All he ever wanted was not to be urged this way and that. To be left to proceed with all the making going on in his head: to fashion the double-bass—a double-bass made a lovely sound—work on the bombs, make another boat, get on with making more clay shapes and the kiln for firing them. True, since the pneumonia allowances were made as not before. They didn't always press in the long holidays for him to go and help the men with the turf and the hay. '...only if you're up to it, Jack,' they said since the pneumonia.

That was maybe clever enough of them for it put him in a spot: if he didn't take a turn with the men, he'd be labelled. Word got around the locality that Jack Normile wasn't up to things. The fact that he was averse to that kind of physical exertion but not to plenty other activity was not fully respected even inside the family. 'Mollycoddle!' Una would taunt.

More brazen all the time, he found on each return from Tubbernagur. Last week she pitched their father's shoes, which had been waiting there for Maggie to polish, straight at his face. She had thought to do it, anyway, but she was a poor shot with those eyes of hers and the shoes had whizzed past to break the Sacred Heart lamp.

'God save us from sacrilege!' Minnie was outraged. 'May God forgive you. I'll call your father to the pair of you.' Very seldom did Minnie make a show of calling on Sean's authority; such summoning of the father was a gesture to indicate the gravity of the issue, although in reality hers was the final word. Everyone knew. But everyone knew, too, that the act of referring to the head of the family had a significance of an ancient nature although no one would ever try to express what.

'You goaded her,' Sean said, having listened to Una's version.

'I wasn't goading her, just saying plain truth, nothing else. I said who could ever put up with a fright like her around the place, a squawker, with no idea how ridiculous she is, trying to be like the silly twits in her magazines. Look at her—sallow, swarthy, and now the specs as well. God! Some people should never be born, people like Dinny Doyle and her.'

'Hold your tongue! How dare you blaspheme!' Minnie was genuinely shocked. 'You'll have to buy a new Sacred Heart lamp between the pair of you. No pocket money until that's done.'

'That's what you'll have to do,' their father agreed. 'I'm disappointed in you, Una.' Then he added, 'In the pair of you. Control yourselves.'

He was holding documents in his left hand and they shook with a small tremor. The ridges were in his forehead; they had already been there when he came in answer to Minnie's call. He was in a hurry to get away from this added strain, back behind his closed door and the sorting of tedious paperwork. He went out with a stoop.

'God will strike you,' Una said, using an expression of Maggie's which really she did not like but was trying out for the effect. She saw it instantly in the deranged look that swept into Jack's face. It told her there was no quick end to the matter: there would be retaliation in plenty. Why do you hate me, Jack? But out loud, for brave measure to keep the balance, she repeated, 'God will strike you!'

'Enough! Silence! Go about your business, both of you. I am disgusted with you.' Minnie was seriously grieved. Such behaviour would not occur in the families of the other teachers she knew nor in the O'Gorman family.

'I was here, Mam, I'm staying here where I am. I was just going to help Maggie with the shoes when he started at me, calling me names and ridiculing.'

Maggie's snort was at the alleged intention: to be in the kitchen just now was Una's only safety.

Jack, bumping over potholes, considered the necessity that required him to cycle all of twelve miles for one measly pound of tomatoes. Duty to parents. Dependence. If a person only had his own money. He didn't like tomatoes. His sister loved tomatoes. There were ways of poisoning selected edibles and presenting them for consumption to hated targets. Roman methods of elimination. Desirable skills. Superior to the Whelan butchery. But impossible. Anyway, would I? Would I ever...? Thady Keane would, or would he, for all his talk? Avoid the occasion of sin. The safest thing for me is to keep out of the way, keep a distance while the holidays last. I'll stay down the glen, work in the dugout. Start another boat.

And my hair doesn't need cutting; could have gone for weeks yet.

Away to the east, the Galtees peaked high. Not always visible, they were remarkably clear today, navy blue, sharp—in fact, you had to say it—magnificent. What a pity it is the sight of them stirs up a sick feeling. And they are bound to for a while yet for they bring it too close. Tubbernagur. At their base —'amid lakes and mountains' as the prospectus had put it. When I'm away from that place, I want to forget it. Too soon, all too soon it will close in again. No escape yet. There is so much I seem to be hating so much of the time. As to that place, there are just two worthwhile blokes. Father Twomey with his study, the fire and books, even letting me bring books home. But not to be boasted about, that, anywhere. Jealousy everywhere. Una at home and, at Tubbernagur, all the mealy-mouths you wouldn't want to talk to about things going on in your head. Except Thady. And he's the other bloke.

He was on the last stony stretch from the hills before the level two-mile run into Poulanara.

There is so much I seem to be hating. Things, places, people. Townspeople, city people, Tubbernagur people—people outside Balnahown. But even in Balnahown there are people I can't stand. Una—enough of her. Even my mother and father, at times. Too much expecting in them. That one at the post office, cold little eyes, always nosing her open pores into everyone's business and pawing the letters in her cubbyhole. Then the gabbing women, the rubbishy yabbering they go on with, the way they collect around my mother after Mass on a Sunday. And it's not just the women you'd want to keep clear of. I'm glad the Whelans are gone but Paddy O'Gorman isn't. Gombeen. Gives you the feeling he's always sizing you up to get something out you. Thousands, they say, but who'd guess it by the cut of him? The same clothes for Mass all the years I remember. Not that I like Sunday suits. It's just the meanness of him; takes it off straight after Mass and there he is behind the counter, serving the Sunday customers in his smeary everday shirt and old pants held up with a bit of rope. As for the smart alecs lining up outside the church wall to flick their fags under the bushes, their plastered hair, the crease in their trousers, the flashy ties they keep on all Sunday for the dance-hall in the evening, flicking and tapping the ash away like Hollywood types—a bunch of shoneens!

Nearly in Poulanara now. Passing the sawmill.

I have to admit I like the sawmill. No doubt about it. I have to admit there are other parts of the town, too, very interesting. Greatly. In fact, it isn't true that I hate Poulanara—totally. I do not totally hate it. There are the garages, the scrap yard, the forge on the far edge. I'd get on with the people working in those places. The empty old houses and some of the back lanes, I like them. Some townspeople seem to like *me*. I don't have to like back. The fiddle teacher—Mam always says violin—the records he gave me and the needles. Pity about his breath. Maurice Neary likes me—and I don't like him—with his big store and all and his dickie-bow. What would they do at home without his calendar for the bulling and calving dates? I heard him saying to Dad I had qualities. There are benefits to being liked: he lets me look around the warehouse and then the odd nails and screws he gives me—in spite of the butterfly collar, the grey oblong moustache and suit to match. Asking for the blue mud, for sure he is, I'll have to do one of him in it soon.

The thriving business of Neary's General Grocery & Hardware had been built on steady prompt payment. The Normiles, frugal, careful shoppers, but regular and paying on the spot, made the bulk of their purchases at Neary's. That the proprietor sometimes indulged Jack derived from this fact.

Jack decided he'd profit by the ridiculous ride for tomatoes. So he went straight to Neary's store where Maurice Neary, in his shiny starched butterfly collar, was busy but yet said hello and put no difficulty in his way when he said he'd like a tea-chest.

'Indeed'n you can have one, Jack—what's it for?'

'To make the next boat.'

When he had the chest roped to the carrier of his bicycle—an awkward job but he was determined—he cycled around to the barber's which was directly opposite the gates of the county council yard. The barber cut Sean Normile's hair every six weeks; he cut Jack's once during each of the short holidays and twice in the long ones. The manager of the county council yard came in and waited his turn while Jack was in the adjustable chair.

'Do you see this gobby fellow I'm clipping here, he's making a boat. All he wants now is the tar.'

This remark from the barber resulted in an interchange of information between the yard manager and Jack which in due time led to Jack's acquisition of a free container of tar. He packed it into the tea chest and re-tied the awkward ropes. There was surely enough tar there for the bottom and much of the sides of the boat. For the rest, he decided, he'd use up whatever dregs of paint to be found in rusting tins in the outhouses at home. His load was heavy, the hill was long, but he didn't mind the angular burden, the knocking container, the rising ground. He'd start on the boat first thing.

He was fastening the iron gate from the byroad into their own boreen when he remembered he had not bought the tomatoes.

Nine

June-July 1942
Una had volunteered out of a mixture of sympathy
for the woman addressed as Mrs de Burca and a wish
to know more about the situation of Proinsias de
Burca himself. All his books she had read; she
respected him through them. Hitherto she had heard
him spoken of only with commendation and had no
idea that he was in dire straits. She had offered to
stay one Saturday night with Mrs de Burca.

From outside it was a cheerless council house in
one of the meagre streets not far from her digs. Mrs
Breen—from Rotterdam, thirty years ago enamoured
of and married to an Irish sailor in the British
merchant navy—had asked 'You all right chilt?' when
Una told her she would be away on the Saturday
night. Mrs Breen had by now answered the door a
few times to Nelson. 'He hass goot manners,' she
remarked after the most recent of these occasions. But
for her youngest lodger to be away a whole
night...well...she felt responsible to Mrs Normile.

'It's all right, Mrs Breen, I'm helping someone
whose husband is sick.'

Poverty was evident from the exterior. The wood
of the door was splitting, the paint peeling; a murky
tattered curtain was askew on the downstairs
window; the top windows were cracked. Inside was a
small cement-floored hall from which rose a dirty
bare stairs.

'Come in, darlin'. You're the fine girl now to do

this for me. They are nice young people at that Irish place but no one else came to me yet from there. They'll maybe come though. I'll go and ask again. I'm worn out, you see.' Without pause, Mrs de Burca's words ran. 'Come on in, come in.'

She was bringing Una into the room with the crooked curtain. An unbalanced table was pushed against one wall. On it were a few empty glass jamjars and an opened tin of sweetened condensed milk, its jagged lid menacing upwards. There were two flimsy chairs. In a corner, the child Gráinne was lying in a cot too small for her; there was neither pillow nor covering. In the corner nearest the back door stood a long old sword.

'He's above. Would you like to come up to see him?'

'Yes.' Una followed Mrs de Burca up the short stairs. The room was entirely bare except for a pile of rags. On this, seeming almost to fill the cramped space, lay Proinsias de Burca, a long big-boned frame. His impressive, quite bald head was near the door. A vast beard grew down over his chest. Apart from him, supine there in an old shirt and trousers, the room was empty.

'This is Una, Una Normile, Frankie, and she has read all your books. She is a great admirer of your writing.'

He made no response of any kind to their visit but continued to mutter to himself in Irish. It was the first time she had been in the presence of an author; for a meeting with one she had wished many a time. This actuality was nothing like what she had imagined.

When they were downstairs again, Mrs de Burca said, 'He gets worse as the night goes on and that is what I find hardest—in the dead hours.' She made tea. 'No cups darlin', only jampots,' she said. She poured some condensed milk into one of the jars, poured tea on top and gave the mixture to Una. 'You'll not like it maybe so sweet but that's the only milk I have.' The child slept. 'Coming on to the small hours he is worst.'

From upstairs came an abandoned roar. It was repeated a number of times. Then followed a tremendous pounding. These sounds alternated and coincided over a long time. The child woke, sat up, but did not cry. It was as if she took the noise as part of whatever existing meant to her. During the vigil Mrs de Burca had smoked a great deal and supplicated 'Jesus, Mary and Joseph!' every so often. Still smoking, she now gave the child some of the cold tea mixed with the sickly sweet milk.

Suddenly the pounding was coming down the stairs. The fine demented shape of Proinsias de Burca burst into the room where they were and rushed towards the back door. He paused near the sword, picked it up, turned it over, put it down again, muttering without cease. Then he went outside. On his return, he again picked up the sword and lunged at the air, not looking at any of them. For interminable minutes he fought the air and then abruptly stood the weapon back in the corner.

'Have a sup o' tea, Frankie.' Mrs de Burca attempted a casual tone.

He still made no response but swept rapidly upstairs, not pulling the door shut behind him.

'That's how it is every night, some nights, over an' over. Tonight is a good night. But I never know how far he'll go with it.'

'Why don't you get rid of that old sword?'

'I've got rid of many things. If it wasn't that it

would be something else. He prowls off sometimes, collecting. I'm telling you. There is always some wicked thing there in the corner. I don't know how much he is doing it because he can't help it or how much it is to frighten me and Gráinne. They say when people go like that they turn against their own. They had him in the hospital and then they put him out. It's a disgrace the way he is neglected, crucified, by all those jackeens that pretend they are running the republic. It's a sorry state for a man like him—an' he's what I'd call young still. It's a sorry story for Gráinne.' The wordless girl had lain down again and seemed to be sleeping. 'I think the child doesn't have much to hope for with her father and mother in the state they are. No chance.'

Upstairs a bellowing had begun afresh.

'Jesus, Mary and Joseph! Grant that he'll settle. I'm worn out with never sleeping. Sometimes he settles after only one go down the stairs. But only sometimes. You feel like cracking up with it, never knowing when it's going to break out again. He can sleep in the day—and God knows he needs to—but I can't: there's the child to be seen to.'

'Does she go to school?'

'Sometimes...but...ah well, 'tisn't regular. And I tell you, she has a good head. No shortage of brains...like him. Ah, but see what can happen...'

A first faint lightening of the night came through the dismal flittered curtain. It was an hour since the fury from above had subsided.

'I'll stay until it's daylight, Mrs de Burca.'

'You were great to come.'

'I did nothing. I'm really sorry about...all of it. I'd have loved to be able to talk to him. There's so much about his work...the background, the dialect...'

'You know the queer thing is I don't speak it and I don't read it. Funny I was the one he chose? Frankie Burke—I got him to give me his name in English and between ourselves that's what I always call him. But I was a good lover and that's why he took to me. I still am...but that's neither here nor there.'

She smiled a little from her weary, weary face.

When she told them at the *Craobh* how she had found things, one of the older members said, 'Maybe some of it is her own doing. It's true Proinsias has not had a fair deal but she is no easy woman.'

And Una kept reliving the harrowing hours of night in the de Burca household, trying to understand something of the fearful cumulative strain on the woman as night followed night, envisaging the dismal future that seemed in store for the child. Images of the slaughter on the Whelan mud floor kept invading her head. 'When people go like this, they turn against their own'—Mrs de Burca's fear. Contradictions not to be unravelled met her. Why, when an original writer like Proinsias de Burca was vital to the language, were there no resources to succour the condition in which she found him? Why had he linked up with Mrs de Burca? Had they anything at all in common? She was warm, direct, certainly—was it really for the reason that she herself had given, that she had been a good lover? And why had she further said that although she still was, that that was neither here nor there?

Why was Una Normile linking up with Nelson Forterre?

Jack's feet had gone through the first boat on its trial

voyage and similarly through the second. With the second, the feet took a little longer to do so, it being something of an improvement on the first model. Maggie described her view of him on successive occasions returning through the fields from the Scagaire River, wearing the wrecked vessels around his waist, pulled up around him, she said each time, like a knickers.

He believed he had learned through trial and error. His main guides were features in encyclopaediae which Sean had bought at one of Paddy O'Gorman's auctions. As well as closely studying these, he had cycled several times to landing jetties on the Shannon to scrutinise what he could in the way of small craft. During the annual family fortnight in Kilkee, he attentively observed the fishing boats, including those turned upside-down on the rocks, and he made friends with the fishermen. He talked boats with Mr Rydall a little but he went silent if Andrew appeared. Andrew had been born to boats, he'd be bound to despise anyone making what he'd surely see as naïve enquiries. Ah for a boat like Mr Rydall's—but that was a very different matter.

This was his third try.

On the left bank of the Scagaire River—the Normile bank—in the span where it was the boundary between Normile land and Whelan land (this last still untended and awaiting legal sorting out), Jack's explosives shot mud, stone and turf sods into the air, silencing a mounting lark and dislodging a jacksnipe from a marshy afternoon doze. The ground hereabouts was more level than elsewhere in the progress of the stream through their own territory and Jack's intention was to widen and deepen the flow of water so that the resulting pool would be big enough to accommodate the latest boat. It required more navigable space than did the two failed specimens. It was still a very small boat, flat-bottomed, covered with tarred and variously painted lengths of canvas. But it stayed afloat and he paddled it in triumph. The measure of his satisfaction and expansion of heart was that he asked Una to come to see it.

He laid the square lid of a Christmas biscuit tin on his fire in the dugout and melted dripping in it. On this, he spread rounds of unpeeled raw potato as he sliced them off and after a while he cracked two eggs on top of them. There was a fork each. They ate off the lid, a side to each. The potatoes were still a bit hard with bits of fried-in grit, the egg whites were transparent in parts.

'Smoked eggs and spuds,' he said.

'It's a great meal,' Una said.

Afterwards he showed her how to use the paddles and took a photo of her in mid-water.

There had been the gritty fry in the dugout, the lesson in managing the boat, the photo. All that was good. She must not show how good. Jack might turn away from that; he had always rejected any ready joy in her. She must watch herself. He had to return to Tubbernagur the week following. They had remained quiet, careful in regard to each other.

She went into his room as always she did when he had gone, hurrying to get there before Maggie or Minnie started the clean-up. Always something to read there. She took the shiny periodical with prints of pictures by famous artists, further American magazines, *Orlando* by someone called Virginia Woolf—what huge eyes she had!—a book about Byron.

'What are you reading there Una? Let me see...Mother of God! where did you come by these? I thought we had finished with this American rubbishy stuff.'

'They're Thady Keane's, he gets them from cousins in America.'

'They're pagan, that's what they are. And let me see that other coloured thing, that periodical Mmm. Some fine churches, Vienna, Italy...ah Saint Anthony...and Saint Francis, good...Rome...but Sacred Heart of Jesus! those naked shameless fat women! They are filthy, a pollution in any house. Here, give me that.'

Minnie had the top of the range pushed back with the long-legged tongs. Quickly she thrust the scandalous pages into the fire and pulled the iron top closed over them. There was a roar of combustion.

'You'll put the chimney on fire!' Sean flustered through the door from the passage, the reverberating roar in his corner behind the closed door having driven him down to investigate. 'What have you got in there? Shouldn't you have the damper shut?'

'Easy now. Take it easy,' Minnie's face and neck were distressfully flushed.

'Easy? You don't look easy. What's going on? It'll crack the bricks.'

'Ah, the chimney is drawing very strongly because it was swept, that's all.'

The fact of naked women on view a few moments before was not to be presented.

The book on Byron had gilt lettering on its hard

cover. It had an acceptable look. Minnie made no assault when she saw Una quietly beginning it. She merely said, as if there had been no outburst, 'Byron. Hm. No great shakes by all accounts.'

In the next couple of days, as Una got through the book, she took care to read it only when out of sight, just in case. It was clear her mother could never have heard of the doings of Augusta and her half-brother or the reactions would have been dire. When she had finished reading, she hid it pending Jack's return and began *Orlando*. This she read in full view.

'Orlando? A nice-sounding name. Italian. Italian names are nice. Music.'

'I don't know many, Mam. But this is a good name...it is.'

'A woman who turns into a man, you say? A fairy story!'

'No fairy story.'

'A joke, then.'

'Maybe. You could say it's historical. I don't know. I don't know if I like it.'

But she had so often wished she had been born a boy. As a girl she was a mistake. Hideous. People continued to say the pity of her streally straight hair and her father and brother so lucky with all the lovely curls. Sallow colour, bony legs with grainy skin pleased nobody. And the further curse of goggled eyes. Had she been a boy, all those things wouldn't have mattered. Look at Thady Keane. Seen at Tubbernagur, he was as ugly as she was, in fact uglier. In no way did he resemble Andrew Rydall. No manners either—he would probably call Andrew Rydall a shoneen. But you had to like him. Those quick jokes. Smart.

'He'd cut the legs from under you with that tongue of his,' Minnie said of Thady Keane, having listened to him while they all traipsed the grounds at Tubbernagur. 'He'll go far. A bit too far maybe. Daring.' And then surprisingly she added, 'But maybe he'll bring Jack out of himself and this nonsense about city people. Thady Keane is certainly city.'

Yes, always she had thought boys got better treatment, were tolerated more. Allowed out to the houses and cottages where people clustered around the open hearth every night, telling stories and all sorts. Boys could go places and not be asked to account for every move. Even got the lick of the custard saucepan on holidays and titbits denied to the girl in the family. They were the first to get a bicycle. Money was put away for when they were to go to university.

June-July 1942
She was going to many places now, accountable only to herself. A huge appetite for doing. For knowing. There was this linking up with Nelson Forterre.

In Dublin, through this Englishman, she was getting to know aspects and levels of life there which she might not have done without him. He had lived in the city now some years, having come with a number of introductions; these had led to work, to social events. Now she was his companion in these last. He seemed to know the place, or so it appeared to her. Through the journalistic work he did, he had even been commissioned to compile a guide to it. Not all the events did she enjoy, was ill at ease in some but, even so, saw them as part of her latest course, a course which could be called simply *Getting to Know*...any university course could equally be called that. Yes, she was getting to know; there were vast amounts yet to be learned. She had taxed him with idle curiosity in wanting to go with her to the *Craobh*: was she herself linking up with him out of insatiable curiosity? Nothing wrong with curiosity, he had said. They were doing very well together on it. There could, of course, be another name for it.

Ten

Loving, hating. Jack would never say loving. Not ever.

They did not describe how they felt about each other. But she thought of it. In spite of the hate, sometimes so fierce, there had been times he let her into his room, even asked her in. Once he asked her when he wanted to show how he had made funny figures for his magic lantern, capering, flickering on their matchstick legs. Caricatures of Thady Keane and others in Tubbernagur; of the entire household: Minnie, Sean, herself, Maggie, Peetie; of Paddy O'Gorman, Maurice Neary, Elfrida Rydall and her parrot. Mocking was one of his constant loves; sometimes you could join in the laugh, other times you detested it. Always new things from him but mocking was always there, ready.

He was excited at his success with the flickering figures and this time she was the only one handy to be a witness. Was that why he asked her in? To applaud? He called in Maggie when she could be heard coming back from the well and clattering down buckets of water in the back porch, and then Minnie and Sean when they came home.

Once he called her in to watch him smoke one of the cigars he had made from brown paper and dried elder leaves. This achievement he didn't want anyone else in the house to know of, but the smell got Sean worried—house on fire, good God!—and he came up to investigate. Sean was much disturbed at the turn of this experiment. Maggie reported later that she had met him coming down the stairs holding the sides of his face, a hand to each side, she said, trying to straighten it out from weeping.

'He'll stop at nothing. God knows what he'll do next for excitement,' Sean said to Minnie. Minnie herself smoked the odd cigarette; Sean smoked his pipe.

She said calmly, 'Ah have sense man, what harm is it apart from the chance of fire? May that be all the cause he ever gives you...'

'And isn't the danger of fire bad enough, not to talk of the degeneracy? At his age. Where did he get the idea?'

'I wonder where now? Not so far away surely.' She was tart.

Because it was one of the times Jack was being friendly, Una felt relieved that the discovery was let go without punishment. That it was so exempt was to be wondered at. Sean had whipped Jack that time when a crack was found in the glass of the new, greatly prized wall clock in the sitting room. Minnie and Sean had bought it in Limerick after the intense exchange of pros and cons, of heated remarks mutually derogatory, and final uncertain truce that preceded the purchase of anything new involving extra outlay. It had been Minnie's choice: it was always Minnie's choice in matters of home improvements. Not that Sean fought her for his choice—he did not pretend to taste—but he objected thoroughly to spending in any way he considered might be unnecessary. It rested with Minnie to demonstrate, victoriously, the virtue of certain expenditures.

Maggie said Jack had cracked the glass doing target practice. Jack denied it.

'Tell the truth!' Sean was angry: the clock was important; truth was even more important. He repeated the injunction again and again, each time with increased fury. Jack continued to deny the crime. Sean's face contorted, his strong tobacco-yellowed teeth showed fearfully. Yet Jack, terrified, held firm. Sean then did what had never been done in the house before: he ordered Jack to take off his trousers. At the sight of her brother's legs coming scraggily down from his shirt tail, Una felt great pity. The whipping was a terrible, unprecedented violence. Jack denied to the end. Una felt that the whipping was more for what her father considered the lie than for the offence of the cracked glass. She believed Jack. She silently held Maggie to be the guilty one. She was hating Maggie for what was being done to Jack.

She had good reason to know Maggie could lie without qualm. She, too, had suffered chastisement from Sean because of Maggie's lying. Not a whipping but a beating with fists. Never had her father as much as slapped her before that.

'Why didn't you bring the matches to the meadow, Una?'

'What matches, Daddy?

'Maggie said she told you I wanted the matches brought out to the meadow.'

'She never told me anything.'

'Tell the truth.'

'I *am* telling the truth.'

'Tell the truth.'

'But Daddy, I *am* telling the truth...I *am*.'

And so it was until the sudden pounding fists. A

bad, bad day. The only time her father had ever hit her, the only time she had wet her knickers with fright and it was fright at his ferocity, and shock that he would not believe her. She had always felt loved by Sean, who said never a word of dispraise against her swarthy skin, lank hair, weak eyes. A great childeen.

Minnie was not in the house when this happened. On her return no one said anything.

That night when alone with her mother, Una gave her side of the story. Minnie said, 'I don't know what to believe.'

The great unfairness, Una felt, was that she could never be proved in the right.

Since the punishment meted by Sean for what he believed to be lies had been so devastating, she did not want to imagine what might have happened had he known about that other much earlier time when she had not yet even made her First Communion. He would surely have judged what had occurred then to be far far worse than lies.

The sixteen-year-old city cousin was sharing Jack's bed that weekend. It was a Saturday so Minnie and Sean were in Poulanara for the weekly shopping. Maggie had gone to the bog with bread and tea for Peetie and the turf-cutters. Jack and the cousin called Una to come into the room. They need not have called so loudly for she was all ears already, wondering why they were taking so long to get dressed and come out. She was glad to go because, since the cousin's arrival, Jack had been in one of his fiercely rejecting moods. 'Keep out. Go away,' he kept shouting at her while he and the other went everywhere, did everything together, laughing a geat deal, the kind of laughing that also said, 'Keep out.

Go away.'

When she went in they were still in bed.

'Come up here.'

They told her what she was to do with her hand.

'It will be milky,' the cousin explained. 'Jack's no good for milk yet,' he said. Loud laughing, but this time she was included.

It seemed huge, purplish. She did not like it. But they were wanting her there. She was an invited important part of their goings-on. She did what they asked—at least what the cousin asked. Jack, sniggering, remained covered by the bedclothes.

It was sticky. Repellent.

'Don't you tell anyone,' they warned. 'If you do, we'll do this to you.' They quickly engulfed her entire head in the worn old eiderdown so that she could not breathe. She flailed desperately, not able to make a sound. She was surely going to die.

When they let her loose they warned again, twice. 'If you tell, we'll do it and we won't let you out. Remember.'

Never afterwards did any one of the three of them refer to this incident. It dwelt however in Una's mind, sometimes receding, at other times horrifyingly reenacted. A mortal sin. Should she die, hell instantly and for all eternity. She made her First Confession, never telling. She did not know how to shape into words what had to be told. Even the continuing awful menace of hell did not help her to come upon any courage even to try.

Minnie was laughing. Although, like Sean, she was too much tightened up around a pack of worries and pressures you might guess at, and sometimes ones you could not imagine at all, unlike him, she often laughed. 'Where's your sense of humour?' she would on occasion say to him, a question which certainly did not help him to find it. You could sometimes hear her laughing from way off as you came back home through the fields, all the house open to the summer air. From the laugh, you could picture her maybe putting a washed milkcan upside down, a little raised against an outer windowsill to let the fresh bog wind sweeten it. She was very particular that everything to do with milk was scoured and clean-smelling: milk could start off TB. Or she might be hanging clothes on the line that stretched all the width of the yard by the ash trees, and laughing at one of Maggie's bits of gossip. It was a good sound her laughing. You felt great love for her, hearing it. You wanted to tell her everything. If the priest were like your mother, laughing like that, you could tell him.

Maybe you could tell him if you kept imagining he was like that. But it would be an impossibility. He was not at all like that. His nose was mottled blue and red, and ended in a ball; the black he wore was going green; a fat sour man you hated to have to be close up to in the smothering confession box.

Yet with a desperate determination to have her mother's summer laughing along with her in the dim stale confessional, she kept the sound somehow about her and brought herself to tell. Years after the event.

There was relief, yes. Certainly a lightening of the dark load. But there was still a guilt, an unease. She was not what she seemed. She was not the childeen her father still called her.

When Maggie was gone on some errand that would keep her away for quite a time, Una told her mother. Not about the finally confessed behaviour with the cousin and Jack, but about accumulated information steadily derived by listening while no one noticed; by endless questioning, especially of Sadie O'Gorman; by forever searching out as much forbidden reading material as she could.

While she spoke she was sitting on the grass by her two valued stones which Peetie had helped her to place, the one from Daly's hill and the other from the bank of the Scagaire River near the Whelans' house. Minnie was on a chair she had brought from the kitchen, darning socks which she took out of an assortment in a large drawstring bag, the thick socks Sean wore when he went shooting or fishing. Una had not looked at her while she talked, she had kept lookng down to where daisies flowered between the two stones. She still did not look at her when, after a stumbling uncomfortable disclosure, she had finished. Neither did Minnie look at her. She began to gather up her mending.

'So that's how it is then,' was all she said. There was no laughing about her. Her face showed a weariness. She did not know how to be with this honest difficult telling, the new aspects of her daughter which it meant, did not welcome this daughter's early knowledge.

Una longed for a warm enfolding in arms. But it had never been her mother's way.

They avoided directly addressing each other for the rest of the day, even when Maggie returned and, later again, Sean.

But Una was glad she had spoken. She felt a cleansing in having done so. Alone in her room that night, when she thought about her parents, she knew she could never have spoken to Sean like that.

She believed she would again hear her mother laughing, from way off.

Of the two, Minnie was the stronger—except for that time when Sean handled Fonsie Whelan—also the more light-hearted. Sean so rarely laughed. When you thought about them, you knew Minnie must truly have more cares than he had. Organising all the workings of the house was a lot, arranging for what Maggie should do, as otherwise Maggie might waste—food, candles, paraffin, soap, beeswax, Silvo, Brasso; Maggie might not properly air the washing, brought in off the line, off the hedge, off the green patch for bleaching; she might scorch garments with the box-iron and its filling of red-hot metal triangle from the fire—all that and more: Maggie always had to be given forceful directions. And then Minnie had to think out the headed lists for Saturday in Poulanara: Neary's, butcher, chemist, cobbler, a line drawn under each. When clothes had to be mended, Minnie mended—but Una was now doing her own. Minnie had to see to Jack's outfit for Tubbernagur—the trunk was huge. For the fortnight's holiday in Kilkee, Minnie had to make sure they would not disgrace themselves in patches and darns in front of the other teachers and their families—Delaneys, Hayeses, Grogans—who turned up each year at the seaside. Nor in front of the shapers from the city who played tennis and had crested swimming suits to show they were members of clubs, and who won prizes for diving the way Una would love to be able to dive.

When it was coming up to October, Minnie had to make sure the chimneys were swept. One of Maggie's jobs. She did it in her oldest clothes wrapped all around in a sacking apron, her head swaddled in a brown cloth. Once the soot was taken away, every item in the rooms was washed or thumped in the wind or hung on the breezy line for, no matter how shielded in old sheets and newspapers, everything had become coated by an insidious sooty residue. Minnie did a large share of the cleaning while monitoring Maggie and Una.

In November, Minnie made the Christmas puddings and cakes to include one each for the relatives further down by the Scagaire River who had only a quarter of an acre. The blood link was on Sean's side but he took no interest, as Minnie, labouring away, did not neglect to tell him. When the time came for the stuffing of the turkey, it was Minnie who did it, a matter not to be trusted to Maggie. On Christmas Eve, Maggie cycled away to her own people in Cloonard, staying with them until Saint Stephen's Day.

Before Easter, there was spring cleaning. In summer, there were huge rhubarb pies to bake for the men in the bogs and meadows: Minnie baked, Maggie delivered.

Neither Sean nor Jack took any part in household matters beyond eating well of meals put before them—only shoneens took part in housework. It would be quite unheard of for them to be involved in any of these things Minnie organised.

Along with them, there was the all-important occupation of her teaching: hours of immense exertion in front of classes, correction of homework, plans overviewed, lessons set out. She was already very tired every day when she and Sean reached home. After the meal—Minnie put finishing touches to what Maggie had part-prepared—Sean settled with the *Irish Independent*, or retired behind a closed door to deal with homework. Minnie sighed and prayed for strength and patience: there were long demanding hours still before she could get to bed. Her prayers for these longed-for benefits seemed seldom effective. Offer it up, she said, there would be rest in the life to come—and a higher place, she hoped, in recompense for the endless striving and straining.

Yet, with it all, Sean appeared more burdened than her. Those ridges and furrows in his forehead...

'Tell the truth!' The greatest emphasis on telling the truth. He, a person sometimes so gentle, had been revealed violent in the pursuit of truth, had whipped his son, had trounced to terror his daughter, in a fury for truth.

Una had never found her father a liar. Her mother frequently was. Work hard, abstain, pray. Her guides. And she abided by them with the exception of not abstaining from lies. An easy liar. Small lies, mostly. Fibs. They were so plainly that, how could she think she was fooling anyone? Pondering it, Una realised that much of the time her mother, indeed, believed her own fibs: she was that kind of inventing person, thinking fast, making up versions and believing them. Sean must also have believed them or else he surely would have beaten her for the sake of truth as he had beaten his son and daughter.

Minnie had a horror, and said it, of death without Extreme Unction. She prayed out loud nightly, after the family Rosary, for the blessing of the Last Sacrament before death. Did she fear being found a battered corpse like Mary Ellen Whelan? Yet she did not desist from fibbing—invention?—nor from exulting in rapid verbal triumphs over her slower-thinking husband.

Other fears she had, revealing flashes of them, not pretending courage: fear of cancer, going bald—a bald woman, Mother of God forbid!—accidents, dotage, decrepitude, the influence of possible bad company on her children. Her talk in general contained many interjections of a prophylactic nature: Sacred Heart have mercy! Lord deliver us! Mother Mary save us! Saints preserve us! It would not be her speech if empty of these and similar invocations. They were necessary to her, her implements to sustain trust, an attempt to abandon all fears to it.

For Sean, a day without the newspaper would be a grievous affliction. He read it with an attention not to be deflected, his feet halfway up the side of the brick arch over the range, his big sugawn-bottomed armchair tilted on its hind legs. Since getting the wireless, he also listened unfailingly to the news. No other sound was permitted at this time. Not even from Minnie. Sean avoided reference to the armed violence and strife in the country in his younger days, beyond a constrained admission, when pressed to talk about these things, that the Tans had given him many a bad fright on the long road as he cycled to his first teaching post, away to the south-east, and back again each day. He did not pronounce on world affairs, for all his assiduous reading and listening, beyond saying 'Ah-sha' as he shuffled back into his slippers, his chair again on its four legs. At election time, he was entirely unwilling to discuss the candidates or the voting, saying only he was a worker, he laboured: a worker ought to vote Labour. For him, there was fear attaching to these matters. Keep clear of politics, a frequent, almost involuntary injunction of his when controversy seemed around the corner.

Further fear Una felt in her father, deep, dark, unspoken. She thought it must be of temptation. Great sin and its worst irrevocable consequences— hell and eternal damnation. Sometimes you could see he was in speechless agony. Did he, also, see a mashed corpse like that of Mary Ellen Whelan? Did that corpse have the pulped features of Minnie Normile?

He always looked easier when he came back from the mountain with the dog, the gun under his arm, the fowler's bag, sometimes quite empty, on his shoulder.

Eleven

May–June 1942

At times Nelson Forterre reminded her of a kind of greyhound. Skin thin over bones. Nose twitching—a perpetual range of invisibilities out there: sniff, sniff? Hunt them out. What is their reality: colour, shape, texture? Nerves at the ready to consider values: select, sample, eat, absorb anything worthwhile.

She said it. 'You put me in mind me of a kind of greyhound.'

'I'm no greyhound. Slow. Slow in deciding. Listen.'

Still munching meditatively a piece of inevitable currant loaf, he said, 'You keep asking me about Penn Reade. Well, when I ask you about what you came from, your people—mother, father, Jack—you go round about, you give me a bit here and there. Jigsaw, you say. I like it. I've been copying you to try to fill in myself. Now about Penn Reade…'

He settled against the bank of heather.

'You see, as I've been giving you some idea I suppose, in my background people were either "one of us"—quotes—or "outsiders"—quotes again. Attitudes were very entrenched.'

They were sitting on a slope beyond the Featherbed. Nearby, their bicycles lay side by side on the path.

'My mother's approval meant a great deal to me, even if I never said it. I suppose I worshipped her, in my inarticulate way.'

Una had a bog orchid in her hand and appeared to be examining it closely.

'She could be devastating in her dismissal of choices I made. In all sorts of things. For example, girls—I did not bring home by any means all the girls, but those I did, well...she was, of course, always strictly polite to them. Only afterwards, the subtle stiletto stabs. Their accent! She is an accurate mimic. Their clothes! She could imitate styles, stances perfectly; the way they held a teacup or ate fruit or handled a knife was—oh, *so* amusing. Ridiculous though you may think it, she had the power to wreck things in this way. Very insidious.'

How could Una Normile ever expose herself to this mother?

'Never direct. Always said as if a joke. Light as light—totally in earnest. Petty, petty things. But that's how it was, still is, in circles like that. People were, are, secretly watched, minutely observed, pigeon-holed, dismissed or accepted according to merciless exclusive codes. I was entirely conditioned by them. What else? Imbued with them. That was the background. The values of my mother, of my family, of the class usages, mores.'

Una had a second bog orchid, the first having crumpled away under her severe examination.

'Trying to get free of all that, I more and more chose counter to the values. My chosen companions were often people I knew they would disapprove of—my mother and the others in the family, I mean. Gestures towards independence. But that is not why I chose to go along with Penn Reade although they certainly disapprove of him—while never having met him.'

'What is it about him?'

'Many things—I've touched on some. But by all standards I was raised on he is what's called a rank outsider. Product of working class and peasant origins. Self-educated to a large degree. He cuts through the petty paraphernalia, the pretensions of class. I first heard him in Manchester. I found him liberating. To me he seemed immensely self-reliant. I think that was the thing that most struck me: his independence of the prevailing powers, politicians, churchmen, the ruling classes. He is his own man.'

'But you are now going for the church?'

'I am—and I am not. Here you see me, over thirty, still searching for what I want most to put my energies into. People can get trapped, have to stick with things purely to earn a crust. I have not wanted to be bound in that way.

'There's a list behind me to date. I didn't want then to go to university. After my father died and there was no money, I went, believe it! into drapery— one of the connections—but I went in at the lowest rung. My mother hoped I'd rapidly climb to executive eminence. I was nineteen—your age. I learned to tie—rather atrociously—cravats for display. Distinctly dim at that occupation.

'The army—another connection, another lowest rung. Made it to lance corporal. Could have done, I suppose, reasonably well but on thinking things deeper, I was not in favour of war. Out I got. No irretrievable disasters, at least so far, and all good for a laugh, ultimately. But my family despaired at this chopping and changing—the eldest should be a beacon of permanence and security. Neither was I a stripling any longer.

'Then journalism—yet a further connection. I have liked it. The training will always be useful. It is one of the reasons I found myself here—although being here has also, in largest measure, to do with Penn Reade. And then the war. I stayed...but, let me underline, not as a war dodger. And the rest...Trinity...thinking of going for the church...on we go. Again a question of values—there have been churchmen in our family for generations, going away back centuries. Anyway, I'm not even now fully sure. Not sure if I want to be taken up in the structures. I'm looking into it...'

'Still? You are thirty-one?'

'I am. But that's what I mean by slow, very late. No greyhound. It has taken me all this time to do some sorting out so far. And I'm not finished with that.'

'Is Penn Reade a communist?'

'No.'

'A socialist?'

'Not that either although a lot of his thinking is in sympathy with socialism—the family of man is his concern. I don't think I would put him in a category.'

'But *you* are falling behind in *your* telling, Una. Come on, I'm waiting.'

'I don't want to stay there at all, Mammy. I'll cycle.'

'Do you think we'd let you do that through the winter? Your health at stake?'

'I'm strong, Mam. You know I am. Look at how often I've cycled to Poulanara for messages and back—in no time at all. So of course I could easily cycle to the convent there, put in the day at school and be back in the evening.'

'You don't want, do you, to fall victim to pneumonia like Jack? We won't hear of you cycling in the terrible winter days.'

'But Mam, I am strong. Jack was not ever as

healthy as me.'

'Well maybe you're not as strong as you think when it comes to what we're talking about.'

'But please—I don't want to have to stay at Neary's the whole time, Mam. Please after Christmas —you'll let me cycle then?'

'After Christmas the weather is worst of all.'

'But then after Saint Patrick's Day, you'll let me after Saint Patrick's Day…'

There was a hesitancy in Minnie. Una pressed on. 'You know I'll be able by then. Daddy knows the way I go through the fields all weathers.'

Sean was not present.

'We're not talking about a ramble through the fields. We're talking about those miles of bad road in the dead of winter, the long hill up.'

'But I'm saying, now, Saint Patrick's Day. Just let me cycle after that. I'd hate to stay all the whole time at Neary's.'

'Aye-yeh, and what will you do so when it's boarding school? Jack had no choice, did he?'

'Well I'd rather stay in the boarding school than down in Poulanara at the Nearys.'

'Going to the convent is to help to break you in— sure we've talked it all out before.'

'I know, but will you agree, so, to the cycling after Saint Patrick's Day?'

A long silence.

'All right so. You're a very obstinate girl.'

Mrs Neary had the palest countenance imaginable. Even her lips, which were narrow and not given to smiling, were almost without colour. Her hair was quite white, combed in a square block, immovable. Large black rims on her spectacles made the paleness and whiteness more remarkable. With the help of Polly, from the poor end of the town, she ran her domestic department: the kitchen at the back of the shop, the rest of the house over it. There, all was specklessly white where white was intended; brushed, burnished and in order to the last detail Meals were of an undeviating punctuality in the scrubbed kitchen with its curtained glass door connecting to the passage and thence, commercial parts.

The whistling Maurice Neary made under his grey small oblong moustache was not a tune, merely a few quick sucks and blows. Throughout the day he produced these sounds every so often except when engaged in eating and drinking.

The paleness of Mrs Neary, Minnie attested, was due to an affliction called anaemia. It accounted for Mrs Neary's slow manner of walking, for the expressionless quality of her eyes. Her face would put you in mind of a mask, Minnie said. Mrs Neary was from the city, a fact she quite frequently referred to, giving the impression that her marrying into Poulanara was something of a benefit to the town. She and Una's mother had known each other over a long period, since, indeed, the time Minnie had emerged from the training course to teach in the town. Because she was an orphan and promising, local authorities had provided her with the course and were instrumental in her initial post. A credit to them, some of the members were heard to say. Mrs Neary was considerably the elder of the two women. Whenever they met, each had always narrowly taken stock of the other's attire and, after marrying, each addressed the other by full married name. Mrs Normile. Mrs Neary.

One Sunday night, the Ford being out of order, Minnie, wearing a weather-battered sou'wester and worn leather coat, returned Una from the rainy windy hills in the pony-trap to Neary's door. When she had gone on her way, Mrs Neary remarked, 'Your mother, as they say, has gone grey, careless and gay. That's what Balnahown has done for her.' She emanated a distinct satisfaction at the effects in her estimation of that district on Mrs Normile. Una did not like the remark. She said nothing.

A great deal was at issue here: the whole matter of what she felt about boggy bleak wonderful Balnahown and dull dreary Poulanara; the countless advantages of the former over the latter where it was decreed she must bide the winter weekdays in the Neary household, so as to get a year's experience of convent education before going to boarding school

She said nothing. She would say too much if she started. Her tongue would run out of control. She would say she hated all the cold cleanliness in Mrs Neary's abode, that the sight of chairs and tables being scrubbed every Monday in the cement-floored yard made her long for bogholes and running barefoot over cowpats; that the white lifeless surfaces, the glint of brass and stainless steel everywhere, filled her with loneliness for the sight of turf ashes gently on shelves and all sorts in Balnahown; that she abominated as intensely the unchanging bluntness of Mrs Neary's square hair as she did Mr Neary's silly cropped moustache and the way it moved like a grey caterpillar when he made that whistle of his every few minutes. Blow suck blow suck blow suck.

'Your mother used to be fond of style.'

She would say nothing.

Saint Patrick's Day did not seem to be quite so far away as it did at the beginning of the term.

Mrs Neary had a tailored brown outfit for Sunday's public appearances. When, each morning she handed Una a bowl of porridge with caster sugar sprikled on top, she had already been to Mass in her weekday good quality navy felt hat and velour coat. Una's bread and butter for lunch was ready in its brown paper bag which she was enjoined always to bring back for the subsequent lunches in the school week.

Jack drew caricatures of Mrs Neary; of Maurice doing his whistle, of the chief sales assistant earmarked to marry their daughter, who had been educated at the Loreto and a College of Commerce in Dublin in preparation for having the business duly signed over to her.

From one to two o'clock, while Una was at the convent school, the serious meal of the day, dinner, took place in the Neary establishment. It was partaken of in rota by all—Maurice Neary, assistants, Mrs Neary, Polly the girl. A portion was put aside for Una. In the interval between this and the evening meal, always called tea, Mrs Neary did not retire to any rest. In her decorous navy outfit she paid a second visit to the church. Her devotions completed, she walked the streets back and then through the side entrance to her living quarters. Entering in this way, she avoided contact with her busy husband, his staff and his customers.

The management of her domestic realm, her quarterly visits to the city to view and sometimes buy subdued high-quality garments, and her twice daily periods in the church—these were what constituted her interests. The maintenance of her husband's well-pressed grey suits, of his starched butterfly collars and dickie-bows, she included in her schedule. She fed him adequately. Beyond this, she exchanged with him per day some innocuous sentences, mostly in the presence of others.

At night, in their stainless bed, she spent a number of inactive hours beside him. When, on her late-afternoon return from the church, she had divested herself of her street wear, she put on an unyielding wraparound overall to supervise and participate in preparations for tea.

Maurice Neary was the last in the household to take his tea. He waited until the shop was closed and the sales assistants gone home. He ate tidily, some reading matter of a business nature propped against the milk jug. Three cups of tea he invariably took, his wife ready for each refill, lifting the pot from where it was kept hot on the stove.

'After tea I'll get them for you, young lady.'

He was referring to the exercise books Una had asked for. Her mother, she said, would settle with him on Saturday when she paid for the other shopping. Between tea and bedtime she read in the kitchen, having already finished her homework in her room upstairs next to Polly's: by this time Polly would have transferred the small portable oil heater into her own room. Tonight she was not reading. She was thinking of Saturday. To do that was good. Every Saturday she went up home with Minnie and Sean; every Sunday evening they drove her down again. To think of Sunday—Sunday evening—was awful.

'Come now,' he said. He had put down his cup precisely and for the last time. In the passage the light was kept thriftily low. Such as it was, the girl

Polly turned it off, going to bed after her time out. He switched on one bulb only in the shop. 'Come here and choose.'

She pointed out her choices. He placed them on the counter and entered their price in the accounts ledger.

'I'll give you a bonus of a pencil.' He reached past her to a box from which he held out a pencil with his left hand. With the fingers of his right hand he made a rapid twiddle on the nipple sprouting beneath her school blouse, immediately going on with markings in the ledger, whistling his whistle. He was older than her father. Odious. The sly speed, the whistling. More despicably odious. She made no sign. To make no sign was to ignore, to deny him any satisfaction; the disgusting thing was too low to have happened. Therefore she took the books, the hateful pencil, and went.

Passing the curtained glass door of the kitchen, she saw the blurred shape of Mrs Neary inside. For the first time she felt a stirring of warmth for the clean bloodless woman, warmth that was however almost instantly swamped in revulsion—from the inflexible, mechanical organisation of Neary domesticity and accounts in ledgers and the altogether unsuspected rottenness that she now knew lived under that, from the sickening vision of Mrs Neary lying in the white white sheets beside the caterpillar moustache.

She could not tell Minnie. This she did not want to tell Minnie. She struck off another day in her calendar as each night she did. She would need no further exercise books until after Saint Parick's Day.

In the meantime she would watch and avoid.

'A wild daffodil, that's what she is,' the youngest sales assistant said. He was sitting on the bridge over the Nara river; his wiry hair much oiled and flattened against his scalp. He was swinging a leg over the water, which at this point was wide, shallow and harbouring oddments of town debris caught on branches blown down from overhead and lodged in the unpleasant sludge. To this, he added the butt of his cigarette. His remark pertained to a girl of about sixteen who was to be seen moving in a lithesome way, up and down the rectangle of pavement outside a shop across from the river. She was wearing a yellow coat which was all the brighter because of the March sun. Her hair, a fine growth, was dressed in many dark ringlets.

Una was surprised, first, at seeing the youngest sales assistant—his name was Tony—sitting where she had never previously seen him, then at his addressing her at all and, further, that he should express himself in such a free way: there was a quality to that quick sentence which caught her fancy. Before this, she had seen him only inside the confines of the Neary establishment where he never said anything to her more than 'How're you?' in passing.

The girl she had noticed a few other times: she visited relatives of hers who lived in that shop outside which she was now so sinuously proceeding up and down. A beauty. To observe her any time was to despair. To look at her now was to be afresh suddenly greatly sad. Sad rather than jealous: no-one could ever be imagined speaking of herself, Una Normile, in such a way. A wild daffodil. He was taking the legitimate fifteen-minutes' break allowed him after he had eaten the lunch provided by Mrs Neary. Una was returning unusually early from the convent because the students had, unexpectedly, been given a half-day to honour the oldest nun's fiftieth anniversary of vows.

'She is lovely,' she agreed about the girl in yellow: nothing a person said would take fron such painful beauty; to try to do it would be stupid. 'But she's not like anything wild. She's a city girl—their cousin from the city.' There was no consolation either in correcting the idea of wildness.

'I know who she is, where she comes from.' It was plain he wanted to know more. That however would have to wait if he wanted to keep his job; the fifteen minutes was almost up. 'Must hurry.'

And he hurried. Una continued in the same direction, in no way hastening to catch up. There she was, bony schoolgirl. If there was anything to be remarked about her, it was surely the schoolboy's overcoat, seviceable and nothing like a daffodil. Jack had outgrown it two winters ago.

In the square, around the raised cobbled centre, there were donkey carts now empty of their loads of turf. The donkeys were getting some rest before the long climb home to the bogs, their owners mostly out of sight, taking a pint in the nearest pub. Dinny Doyle's father was just going in for his. Dinny was sitting in the cart, looking vacuously in front of him.

'Hello Dinny,' Una said. Beyond that, it was hard to know what to say to him. In Balnahown, when you passed him, standing solitary, at the gable end of his house, you called out, 'Hello Dinny!' Sometimes he said hello back, brightening, seeming glad of the greeting. Sometimes it was as if he did not see you for he showed no trace of response. But you said hello anyway.

'The poor unfortunate,' Minnie would remark. 'God save us from such misfortune! We should be thankful.'

'Ah-sha,' Sean said once, 'isn't the way of describing him in Irish *"duine le Dia"* and don't we all know that means "a person with God".'

The Doyles sold turf in the town; they had two cows, two goats and every year a clutch of chickens. Dinny's mongrel dog was usually near him; very often he put his hand on the dog who equally often pushed against him companionably and licked the approaching hand. Jack, who used to say Dinny Doyle ought not have been born, could sometimes latterly be noticed stopping and talking to him in the holidays. Jack, sometimes latterly, also talked to Una, who according to his earlier view should not have been born either. The dog was with Dinny in the cart today, the pair of them sitting on a bundle of empty turf-bags. Dinny brightened in his unforeseeable way when Una greeted him.

He said, 'New collar,' and put his hand on the dog's neck. 'Bell,' he said and jingled it.

The dog smiled as dogs do. The March sun showed in great clearness the dribble down Dinny's chin, the dried deposit of successive dribbles on the front of his old jacket.

''Tis a great new collar for your dog, Dinny.'

He looked sideways at her, holding out his other hand, back upwards. 'Sun,' he said. The hand had grace but it was very pale. Delicately made. 'Happy,' said Dinny.

The girl with the yellow coat and ringletted hair was coming into the square, accompanied by two of her relatives.

'I sometimes give him liquorice,' Minnie had said. 'Two sticks of it I gave him the other day, the poor misfortune.'

Jack, moody because Tubbernagur was looming yet again, had taken her up. 'People like Dinny don't know they are trapped. Maybe...' There was a difference now in the tone he used, speaking of Dinny.

Maybe what? Jack didn't go on and Una did not ask. The last day before another return to Tubbernagur. A dangerous time. To pester with questions might switch him back to a black exclusion of her. She feared that. She also feared the reprisal that could ferment in herself.

But maybe what? Maybe...we can be happy? Covering the last part of her way to Neary's door, she was saying it to herself, Maybe we can be happy. This year Saint Patrick's Day fell on Sunday. Sunday coming.

'I'll be cycling past your house every day come Monday,' she had said to Dinny by way of goodbye.

Maybe more often than she knew, Dinny was able to be happy...maybe people like Dinny could be happy. The dog had smiled.

Maybe the girl in the daffodil coat might one day have a child like Dinny. That would make for fairness. Maybe Una Normile could make up for not looking like a wild daffodil. Maybe there are people—boys, young men—who could be interested in you for things other than your looks. Clever fellows like Thady Keane. She did not really believe it as she caught a reflection of her schoolboy's overcoat going past Neary's window on her way to the side entrance.

But—and oh joy!—she would not have to walk

through that entrance any more, come Saturday evening when she went home with Minnie and Sean. Saint Patrick's Day this year was a thing in the immediate future about which to be exceedingly happy. No maybe to that certainty. She would whizz on her bike down the long hill, the Galtees in the far distance; she would not care a bit about the heavy pull back up home in the evenings.

Twelve

June–July 1942

The vicarage was spacious. Built in Tudor style, impeccably kept. There was Nanny Cairn, the cook, two village girls to help.

The parishoners liked the Reverend Paul Forterre. Easygoing. Not at all pressed with wanting to be a bishop. His little addresses from the pulpit made no strenuous spiritual demands. He liked the outdoors. On the great-aunt's estate was plenty game and fishing.

'In fact,' Nelson said, 'I think he was like your father—as you describe him.'

'Ah no—maybe that liking to be out of doors but…well, as to religion…there seems to have been no hell tormenting your father. Your religion sees hell differently. With us, it's hard, it's impossible, to get away from it. My dad is full of the fear of it. With us all it is…has been…except with Thady Keane, a roaring reality.'

'But take away the trappings—'

'Can you? Can that ever be done?'

He carried on as if she had not interrupted, '…take away the trappings, those two men could be friends.'

'No way to do it, is there? Your father is dead. But maybe I understand what you mean…you're talking about the accidents—birth, where you find yourself, the beliefs you're born into and…so on…'

'Yes, take away the trappings—I'm interested in

that. Getting down to the essential person. My mother now…'

'Ah, your mother…'

'Poor thing, it's a lonely time for her, this war. Miles away on her own in Cornwall. She loves company. That mixture of bloods in her…'

'…in you, too, don't forget.'

'More diluted. But in her, I think the mixture makes for a notable complexity. I remember her as being so often a creature of electric changes.'

Charm and kindness she had in plenty for the parishoners. But she detested any what she called stepping out of place on their part, any forwardness. In planning and contriving for the correct externals of her own family, she was imaginative, resourceful, and then made fun of her efforts. A sense of the ridiculous but also many fears. These last had greatly to do—in spite of self-ridicule—with loss of face, with the diminishing effects of poverty such as that in which 'the lower orders' had to live.

'How too awful to be like them. One would kill oneself rather than it! Find an heiress, Nelson, who will swoon with love for you. Enslave her. Marry her, for all our sakes.'

He told Una that however much a joke she made it, it was very definitely also a wish. Having burst out in this way, she laughed. And then she sighed. A long sigh.

It was, indeed, too soon for her to have recovered from her husband's death. Nelson, nineteen, and quite, quite unable to know what to make of himself. And the others to be seen to. If only he were of a decisive masterful caste like his great-uncle von Kleber, she, they all would regain the fortune so foolishly lost by lovable muddling Paul. But Nelson had, as yet, shown no aptitude for money-making. Still, one never knew. She continued to hope. 'My darling sonny.'

Anyhow, something had to be done with him quickly. No longer could his playing about with ideas be indulged. This had got him nowhere: no academic clout, no clear decisions. His sojourn in Poland and Russia had not improved his moodiness. His voiced sympathy with the workers could now be applied. Besides, let it be faced, many a title moving in coveted society had achieved such currency through trade. Down through history as everyone knew, rich traders aiding needy powers—royalty and aristocracy—had reaped honours. Never forgetting the financial expertise of Great-uncle von Kleber—that 'von' was skilfully manoeuvred, an honour bestowed in return for monetary facilitations.

For Nelson's sake, she would surrender pride—had she not had to do it already? This time, she would turn to Sir Philip—a place, any place, could surely be found for Nelson in the business chain Sir Philip so competently administered. Chairman of the Board—things can be arranged. Here in England, Nelson might yet show a business acumen as had the great-uncle in Europe.

And thus Nelson was duly placed in Sir Philip's sales concerns, in no less a section than the neckwear department of an emporium in the large chain.

'I wasn't the least bit good at it,' he had told Una. 'I don't think I ever sold more than a dozen items. It didn't last long. And I learned some things, amongst them, as I think I said, how to tie a variety of knots. Much as boy scouts do. Brilliant achievement. The next phase—I'm recapping—was the army. Again introductions helped, at least to set the machinery in motion. But no jumping rank. Started at the bottom, learned how to tie some more knots.'

No happier in the army but stuck it a while; then thinking out the sequel to such a position—support of war—departed the ranks.

'What *are* you to do, Nelson? What are *we* to do with you?'

Her eldest, her first joy of maternity. In the morning, Nanny Cairn sometimes allowed him to run to her from the nursery, in his childish nightshirt, and touch with wonder her astonishing mass of hair. It was entirely grey now. Mrs Forterre said no one would want to touch it. Nanny Cairn had long gone. The others had found occupations. He still came to her but in a cloud of frustration.

'Why? What is it you do *want*, Nelson?'

'I'm afraid you have a late developer in me, mother. I'm still searching. But don't worry, I'm not coming to scrounge. I will always earn. Just still looking.'

While still looking—and listening—he had heard Penn Reade one night in Manchester. At the time, he was quite enjoying his job as reporter. Reade, when he talked with him, did not at all denigrate his zigzag, apparently indeterminate course to date. He agreed there was a need to search: not everyone was satisfied to go on a railway line from A to B. He, indeed, applauded what he spoke of as Nelson's integrity in admitting to himself that job after job was not satisfactory to some deeper wants.

Hearing about it all, Una felt it would be very frightening to be thrust into the ambience of Nelson's people.

But she liked, too, the pictures evoked of much of

his background. Some had suggestions of the Rydalls, some were altogether grander than the Rydalls, who, for all their elegant speech and cultured manner, never really bothered about clothes, nor appearances, nor putting on a fine style, and lived in a house crumbling in parts with many of its contents neglected, even battered. Nelson was right about the trappings—without them, it was quite likely their two fathers could have hit it off. And she could well envisage the Reverend Paul Forterre, as evoked by Nelson, and the Reverend Eustace Rydall being much in sympathy. Mr Rydall and Elfrida would have been entirely happy at the scene Nelson conjured up of his very young self with his sisters, younger still, wearing sailor suits, sitting in the dog-cart decorated with flower garlands—flowers from the vicarage garden—on the shafts and wheelspokes, a bell on the donkey's neck, all for the village fête.

The more splendid houses Nelson told about, where he'd been invited to this that and the other society event, set off the imagination: the way things were done, the procedure accompanying the serving of banquets, the etiquette observed.

The ministrations of valets and chambermaids at weekend house parties. The assurance of the privileged, born to a position which made them the bestowers of largesse, the recipients of the services of pyramids of staff. Of course it was wrong that a privileged section should hold sway—think of the English dispossessing the native Irish and lording it over them. Think of the privileged, anywhere, in the midst of deprivation. But in spite of yourself you imagined yourself into the exhilaration of power, the intoxication of it. Lucifer the seducer, power-crazy. This was madness. This had to do with destruction, with wars. All humans had madness in them. Bible stories had it right. Angled mirrors.

Anyway Nelson had searched out and away, gone another journey, was interested in a different sort of power. Should any windfalls blow his way from what he had left behind, a few of those from well-stocked territory, should they ever come—was it unprincipled to avail of them? No ill-gotten gains? A matter of equitable distribution.

Thirteen

Jack had been right. Nothing like the frolics in *Girl's Own Paper*.

The second week in Marymount College proved even more abysmal than the first. Before coming, Una could not have believed a person could feel so lonely.

The greatest happiness had always been in the bogland: rushing against the wind across *fionán*, galloping barefoot upstream in the shallow brown river, climbing ash trees to hang, knees hooked over a branch, and see the upside-down world.

The boarding school spaces cramped the chest and set up a great ache there for wide open reaches under speeding clouds. The only thing to help was to attempt concentration on all the new material to be learned. Not to do it was to be ill with loneliness, with hate for the dismal passages, the cloistered odours.

Sixteen narrow beds in her dormitory. The fat girl burgeoned over the edge, so her bed was put flush to the wall for at least some support. She had a steady supply of goodies which her parents brought in person so as to stow them in her locker without the intervention of authority to which postal delivery was subjected. They owned a fancy goods shop. In the dark, she was to be heard munching and crunching, tormenting the hungry. Very occasionaly, her arbitrary favours meant that a chosen few shared a fragment of the luxuries. Una was not one of the few: she did not take readily to fat anything.

More than from hunger, she suffered from the cold. In truth, there was food enough to stave off starvation—dull, but there. Bread and tea twice a day, bread and milk once, a dinner of boiled mutton, cabbage, potatoes when classes finished at four o'clock. The only variation was the substitution of turnip sometimes for cabbage and the addition of rhubarb jam at teatime on Sunday. Rhubarb was an easy crop. You welcomed what was put in front of you. The yeast bread was good, made daily by lay nuns in the convent bakery. Fragile white circular wafers, intended for Transubstantiation in the awesome central focus of daily Mass, were also made in the bakery.

The cold was unrelenting. An aloof frozen moon shone through high uncurtained windows and throughout the night in the arctic dormitory the blood in your feet was ice. The fat girl snored. You could wish to be fat and to snore through the iron cold night. In the preponderance of stone passages there was no waft of warmth. The refectory was but an extension of these, its only advantage over them being that there you were allowed the legitmate if hasty swallowing of food.

To Una, stillness of a certain nature had always been significant. At home in Balnahown, there was that stillness which so often came with twilight, the countryside so quiet that any small sound could be heard, it seemed, for miles: the call of the *gowreen roe*, the curlew, the clank of a milk tank in a farmyard, the rattle of a donkey cart on some stony boreen. At such times, an essence came out of the land and down out of the sky, diffused in the wide air, making you want to be dissolved in it, your unpleasing body absorbed into the mysteriousness of it, along with the haunting corpse of Mary Ellen Whelan flashing you never knew when in your head, the ugliness of the thing with the city cousin, the recoil from Maurice Neary's twiddling finger, all the hates. You were alone at these times.

In Marymount, you were never alone but yet, unexpectedly, you found stillness—of quite another kind and yet the same.

From without, the chapel was unremarkable, a small narrow cement-coated structure abutting at right angles from the main body of the college. Inside, nuns in their stalls, one behind the other, ranged at each side of the narrow nave; novices down the centre in their white veils, and younger still postulants in their net-frilled caps nearest the altar. In one small transept, the boarders of the college; in the transept opposite, the waifs and orphans of the redbrick industrial school with whom no contact was allowed.

Your early reaction to the chapel was one of guilty resentment. It was a place you were monitored into very early each morning, barely awake after little sleep because of the cold, and wanting nothing more than to sleep and sleep. But after a time it increasingly affected you in another way.

It seemed there was a quality here nowhere else in the college. It seemed compounded of many things. All together they became a richness. In the bare structures of Marymount the chapel was a place of richness—that pleased. Soothed. Nourished. The colours in the stained glass window high behind the altar; the chasubles of the priest and *their* colour which changed according to the liturgical significance of the day and which, for special feast-days, had been unsparingly embroidered in embossed designs of different hues and gold and silver thread; the profusion of flowers always fresh from convent garden or greenhouse; the patterned light of adroitly placed candles; the permeating fragrance of incense; the warmth—the one centre of warmth; the music of the organ and carefully modulated choir; the Latin in its ritual flow. And with all these, the stillness. The rarified sounds contributed to it. It was the most important element of the special quality, yet its importance grew out of the abundance created by all the rest. At certain parts of ceremonies, an almost complete, eternal stillness which seemed like a unification into which were taken, and turned into a peacefulness, the anxieties, rancours, inequalities and pettinesses of the daily moil. You forgot that Mother Immaculata's head never bowed in humility and that the industrial school with its waifs and orphans was an institution strangely apart, untouchable—all God's children, inexplicably separated. In no other chapel or church, not in Balnahown, Moygrane, Poulanara nor in the city, had you found this particular inclusive stillness. It became a secret solace. Brief. For the daily moil certainly returned swiftly and had to be met.

Every activity monitored.

You made your bed after Mass and breakfast. All in silence, a silence different from that in the chapel: their was a grimness to its imposition. Then, along with the others, you took your books to the path which bordered the square of grass. There, your breath an instantly freezing clump, you marched as fast as possible with your open book, learning off by heart Aodhagán Ó Raithile or Seán Clárach Mac Domhnaill or Tadhg Gaedhealach Ó Súilleabháin and others for the dread Mother Immaculata whose petrifying sarcasm you would meet in fifteen minutes' time. A very large classroom, composed mainly, it felt, of winter draughts. Four giant windows, four doors, one at each corner. In the middle of one long wall, a tiny fire. No other heating. But while you still marched outside with your open book, there were sometimes amazing sunrise skies against which configured most strikngly the bare black trees of the orchard.

Work hard, abstain, pray. Minnie's maxims but here most exigently endorsed. Mother Immaculata did not expound these: her delegates did. Mother Immaculata seemed to move in an aura of unreachable isolation, that of the absolute ruler. She did not show the humility of posture in prayer, common to other nuns. The morning introductory prayer when boarders and day girls, all, assembled before classes, she rendered in a hard staccato which stabbed crucially at any struggling courage. She appeared to be forever taken up with affairs of supreme importance, leaving lesser matters to her inferiors in the convent hierarchy. They defined existence by the life to come, constantly insisting rewards there to be in proportion to the rigours of the earthly span. The hard work centred on good examination results which, while equipping candidates with entry to a livelihood, would also ensure the continuing worthy reputation of the college. They did not say it quite this way but the older girls knew. An outstandingly successful pupil might receive mention in the national newspapers; local newspapers gave details which could repercuss profitably. The older girls knew.

Sports were of no importance. They entailed the showing of thighs and other unmentionable facts of female anatomy and functions. Girls had no thighs, therefore nothing at their apex. Nor any breasts. These parts were ignored at all times, including biology and hygiene classes. Eliminatory processes got a token reference—tension paramount, an embarrassed flicking through the colon, the kidneys. Reproduction of the human species officially remained an ironcast mystery.

'An extraordinary thing!' The older girls were agog one day, 'There are to be gym classes!'

Never had there been the like. But, they said, Mother Immaculata had made the unmistakable announcement to the prefects. It had, without any doubt, they went on, to do with Saint Ita's. That place—rival convent in a neighouring county—was getting very good exam results lately and it also went in a lot for games.

So now gym blouses and tunics were issued, the cost to be on the quarterly bill home. The girls were not yet allowed even to try them on. The reason for this soon manifested itself. The shortness of the tunic was to be marvelled at.

'Thighs!' the girls screeched, holding up the garments by the shoulders and looking at one another. The gymnastics instructress, newly engaged, looked incredulous as her raw material presented themselves in the concreted yard, wearing gym blouses and tunics *over* their everyday heavy long serge uniform. Of thighs there was no evidence.

'What's this nonsense?'

'We were told to, Miss.'

'Take off those… those…encumbering uniforms!'

'We were told not to, Miss.!

'I have never seen anything so ridiculous.

Gymnastics are to free you, loosen you up, not bag you and clog you in extra layers. We may as well not have this class.'

However, they did, working through a stilted range of sweaty jerks.

''Tis idiotic,' the outspoken older few said, 'Immaculata never meant any real exercises anyway. She's just doing this *mar dheadh* that we're not being outdone by Saint Ita's.'

The process was repeated the following Saturday—a wet day—in a typing room, the desks with their typewriters having been pushed back to the walls. The instructress's mouth clamped when she saw the reappearance of stuffed shapes in double skirts. To the class this time she said nothing, but afterwards must have presented her case to the operative power with exceptional persuasion—a rumour was afoot that her father had been a divil of a colonel. With the British, in the colonies. That she was so good at the job because of the way he drilled her. However unfounded the rumour—and in view of Mother Immaculata'a strongly nationalistic exudations (direct propaganda was too blunt for her style), it seemed so—there followed from Mother Immaculata's formidable lips no straight reference to outlooks on the nature of physical training. Instead, there was merely the issuing of an edict via delegates: thenceforth, the prescribed attire for gymnastic class was gymnastic blouse and tunic only.

After the first tearing loneliness, a rhythm had become habitual. There came, to succour, the saving stimulus of curiosity and its consequent movement of work enjoyed, the pleasures of learning, successes, friendships, recreation, laughter—all gathering together the swift years.

June–July 1942
    'They marked you, those years,' Nelson said.
    'They did. Indeed they did.'
    'Indeed they did. Profoundly, I would say.'
    'Yes, that is true. I owe them much.'

A brown coarse habit; an unnaturally parchment-coloured face, its dark eyebrous arching out of sight under the rigid coif; glinting metal frames on the glasses behind which eyes appeared unpleasantly big; a smile which was a drawing wide of lips from teeth irregular and beige. Breath from such a mouth could not be other than an affliction. At any slight body movement a clank of the long hugely beaded rosary attached to the leather belt.

    'You would be redeeming these little creatures from the wilderness of paganism.'

    The photos showed black children in a variety of ages and expressions.

    'Each baptised soul would be adding to your actual grace, to your hope of peaceful death, of salvation in the hereafter.'

    A sister of the Franciscan order. Ugly. Her companion in religion—nuns always travelled in pairs—who remained silent, stood to one side of the final-year class, her hands swallowed in the immense sleeves meeting across her stomach. Ugly, too. Jack had lacerated Una with her own ugliness. She saw the ugliness of these religious figures before her now, and dismissed it. She got a whiff of the breath and, yes, it was vile to anyone near it. She dismissed it also. These, she had read in books for spiritual edification, were but some of the accidents—meaning outward features—which frequently coexisted with inner sanctity. These ungainly, unsightly women in rough cloth with heads, under the weighty veil and unyielding coif, kept in a more or less permanent downward slope of modesty, were instruments of the higher life. So affirmed her reading from the holy shelves. To this she had given much thought.

The final year. Other missionary orders sent out recruiters, feelers in pairs, so that a few times a year Marymount College had indeed felt them.

While not actively disparaging them, the teaching nuns in the college gave off an air of something negative in their regard: these recruiting nuns were intrusive; they interrupted the rigorously structured timetable, taking from the planned daily quota of lessons; they—and this was a most serious consideration—were there for the sole purpose of working on impressionable young minds, enticing what could be valuable material for the home ground. Marymount College also needed recruitment in both academic and domestic ranks. Una had had intimations that she herself was a target for such recruitment.

Mother Immaculata did not personally offer hospitality to these visiting sisters. Such an obligation she delegated to others, the aura of imperial duties exonerating her from involvement with them. She was not the woman for teacup trivia. Neither was she a person to speak of God or bonuses in a life beyond the grave as an incentive to gaining promising students for the college teaching staff. Her God must have been a gaunt power, not to be broached for comfort or guidance. It was unimaginable that Mother Immaculata would turn anywhere for such. When the bishop, in his purple and self-importance, came from his palace outside the town, it was with evident, if silent fury she made token motions in haughty observance of the decreed obeisance and kissing of the ruby ring. Her head never bowed nor did she ever initiate prayers; this duty was also passed on. Her continuing condition before her pupils seemed to be one of entrenched unyielding-ness to any authority in terms of daily life. You did not think of her as a woman, the physical woman she was, an overweight, ageing woman, lumbering on misshapen surgical boots along corridors. Rather, you thought of her as a solitary, irreversible force, kept on her inexorable, commanding feet, it seemed, by some unquenchable anger, the reason for which there continued divers apocrypha.

That she should suggest taking the veil to be a desirable course for a student was something you did not envisage. You could think of her more as an empress, sending out fleets of galleons to conquer and rule. It was with surprise, therefore, her senior class heard her remark one day, dryly, and as if it were of no particular point: 'There are advantages to joining a religious order. Energies can be usefully employed there. The order of this convent is...commendable. A few of you might think in that direction...Miss Lacy, maybe, or Miss Collins or... Miss Normile?' She used 'Miss' like this, they knew, when she wished to emphasise most her distance from them. Even so, the mention of your name had something of the effect of an acknowledgement, very rare and grudging at that, from Jack in earlier days.

Those not sitting the Department exams had aleady gone home on holidays. The dormitory was almost empty. It was bedtime but the windy summer evening was still quite bright. Una had stood on the wide window ledge above her bed in an attempt to stop, with a wad of paper, the rattle of the frame: no help, such a racket when you wanted to get some— forbidden—last minute revision-flicking done in bed. Smuggled books under the pillow. From her unusual vantage on the ledge, she could see the figure of Mother Immaculata standing in the grounds, her black habit and veil held close because of the wind. Standing thus she, so normally impregnable, showed somehow vulnerable. She was gazing at the redbrick building of the industrial school. Why? Could she possibly be thinking of the gulf between the lives in it and a palace housing a single individual, garnished in pompous purple and a valuable ring, who uttered turgid sentences and who was taken about in a large chauffeur-driven car? Christ on a donkey in his seamless garment. All God's children. Could she? Or were you just hoping she might be? You were wishing you could have known her better, this enigmatic creature. But you would not so know her in the time left. The unknowable, powerful creature who had so marked you over the years.

June–July 1942

'I'm glad to hear all your talk of nuns,' said Nelson. 'For all my going about, I had, up to now, only read of these things. They marked you, these things.'

'Yes.'

'They did.'

'True. They were…deep times.'

Were a person—that person being herself, Una Normile—to do it at all, it would be for what required the greatest demand. Which order required that? Teaching orders did not do so. In many ways frugal and disciplined, yes, they were that, but their way was not a total relinquishing of worldly connections, not a full submission to the ascetic way. They had an eye on money, on social grading: why else, in this immediate order she now knew best, the existence of an untouchable colony, the industrial school?

The orders of the visiting missionaries? More exacting, probably, but neither were they the full measure. None had come from a leper colony. A life devoted to such a place, that surely was one of greatest demand: how could one ever face existing—eating, drinking—in daily confrontation with that rotting flesh, how minister to it? Was that it, a nun in a leper colony?

Visible success. Good job. Climb up, up. Top salary. Plenty for beauty treatment.

Una Normile is one of the golden creatures on a sun-flooded beach. Brilliant nails. Plucked eyebows. Glossy permanent wave. Eyelashes astonishing in mascara. Peach-smooth skin.

Later, in the nightclub, her clinging satin undulates to one of those jazzy tunes Thady Keane had records of. Her partner, in evening clothes, is alive to her compelling curves. The mad fever of something that is to happen soon. And so it will be, day after day, night after night. Urgency of power, triumph of seductions. Event upon event. A kaleidoscopic life…

And what about the mad?

A couple of times a year, the Sunday crocodile passed the county asylum, a mile outside the town. There were no screening trees but clearly to be seen figures of the inmates, pressing against the barred windows, five or more to each one. Una did not wish to look and yet found herself looking in horrified attraction. Leprosy. And then lunacy, idiocy—even more than leprosy, she felt these to be the severest maladies: the collapsed mind, the incomplete brain. The killers of Mary Ellen Whelan. The forever alone-ness of Dinny Doyle. Images of the corpse, of the murdering brothers, rushed upon her with reinforced effect. To think of the accumulation of crazed misery, caged within the barred windows, was to be overwhelmed by a weakness as if you were breaking to pieces.

This final year in the crocodile from Marymount, the crowded windows wrought on her to such a degree that her companions said, 'Una, what ails you at all?'

They put her sitting down on a tussock by the roadside. She said nothing. Inside herself she was saying, 'Please let it not be caring for the mad.'

Yet, if that were the call, heard with sureness, she would—would she? could she?—answer it.

'Please let that not be the call.'

Una Normile, a golden creature on a golden beach...the envy of the dance floor...the urgency of a power that set men beside themselves...triumph of seductions...

Total silence. It could be behind high excluding walls on a declivity in the Appenines or behind walls of the same kind in a city slum. The place would not matter once the choice was made, the commitment given. Total cutting off, utter silence. The moment by moment exigence of an unremitting purification, not as selfish achievement ensuring a personal place in Paradise, but as an endowment—according to all the teaching, grace from such a life was, in some miraculous uncomprehended but promised way, to be bestowed upon others.

Enclosed orders were surely the most exacting? And yet, caring for the insane...

Oh no! not *it*, please.

Were a person to do it at all, a person would become which one of these—carer of lepers, of the mad, a Carmelite?

...swooning beaches...the savouring of seductive powers...the male in thrall...

June–July 1942

'So you, too, have been searching,' Nelson said.

'That is true.'

It was then she showed him the poem. 'The Quest' was the title she had given it.

'I wrote it in Balnahown—after coming to a decision. I haven't yet finished all the telling, though...'

Fourteen

June–July 1942

Women liked Nelson. All ages. She was finding this out.

'Ah Nelson! There you are! When are you coming to demolish strawberries and cream in your inimitable style? You have been neglecting me. I'm here checking on my other Trinity admirers who—let it be understood—are faithful. There will be a couple of them coming for Sunday luncheon—will you join them?'

Then the speaker paused as if she had only just noticed Una. They had been crossing Front Square when the woman with grey hair dyed saffron—the reality showed more than she probably knew—hailed him from the dining hall steps. He said, 'Ah, Mrs Riverdale. This is Una. We are good friends.'

A certain something occurred in Mrs Riverdale's face but she continued in the same high carrying voice. 'How do you do…then of course,' turning to Nelson, 'you must bring Una, too.'

He said for both of them, 'Thank you.' It did not occur to Una that he should have asked whether she were free to go. Not until later, much later. That this should be so indicated something.

'Usual time, then?'

'Oh, how delightful!' Podgy fingers with many rings flicked at him.

Old enough to be his mother. Flirting at the top of her affected voice. Watching her, Una felt sure she had been unwillingly invited despite the jollying front.

Many other women. All ages.

Minnie was away on a retreat. Never before had she done such a thing, nearly a week sleeping away from Sean, sleeping away from the house on her own. That she had gone was surely an implicit measure of her latest attitude to duty: they could fend without her for a few days, surely—there was Jack moving into his finals, Una finished at Marymount. Minnie was therefore in a hostel for religious with women of miscellaneous ages. They had in common their alma mater, the goal of redemption—the priest officiating at the retreat was a Redemptorist—and an amount of small talk. The talk could not be indulged, however, until the days of essential silence had finished when, most likely, a charitable colouring would be redemptively dominant.

'Una, do you know where's Maggie?'

'Is it your tea you want, Daddy?'

'I'm asking you, do you know where's Maggie?'

'I'll get it for you now, Dad.'

'But do you know at all where she is?'

Truth. Sean's passion for truth made side-tracking dificult. Truth would tell that Maggie was at that moment carefully easing her bottom down the lowest part of the sloping roof of the shed at the eastern gable-end. The roof slanted from immediately underneath the ledge of Jack's bedroom window. In that room was Thady Keane, laughing, ready for possible confrontation. Jack had gone a few miles away to procure extra fishing tackle.

Una staggered.

'O—o-oh! My ankle again—that's the second time today; I hurt it when I jumped from the tree yesterday. Give me a hand, Dad, and…ah, there's Maggie for you now…'

Maggie was advancing around the corner of the house carrying a bucket. A bucket was always a useful object. Unquestionable in certain issues. She was going in the direction of the privy which Sean, unaided, had built years back, a matter of pride. No running water. Sluicing had to be done with buckets or basins of a Jeyes' Fluid solution..

'Daddy is wanting his tea, Maggie.'

'I'll be getting it now, Mr Normile, in a minute.'

Sean, in fact, had made no mention of wanting his tea. There was a particular look on his face, the same look as it showed that Sunday, a long time since, when Una had weaved her way through the men and boys listening to the hurling match.

Thady, having executed a rapid physical man-oeuvre, preferable to confrontation, was now to be seen coming in a leisurely way from the direction of the fields west. As he came nearer, a soft-covered book was to be noticed thrust into the pocket of his jacket.

'Ah hello, Mr Normile,' he said easily, smiling the while at Una, 'I've been reading up about the grouse and pheasant. Maybe you'd like to have a look at this.' He pulled out the book and offered it to Sean. 'Got it secondhand the other day.'

'Ah-sha that's one I saw long ago.' Sean did not look at him as he spoke. There was a constraint in him. It was evident that the aplomb of this friend of Jack's did not suit him.

As if quite unaware of any awkwardness in the vis-à-vis, Thady went on, 'Well, of course, there is probably not a thing you don't know about all the wildfowl around here, anyway. Me, I know nothing.'

'I'm sure you know plenty about a lot of other things.'

'The tea is ready now, Master.' Maggie came out to tell Sean. Between her and Thady, there was no sign. Sean did not invite Thady to come in to the table. Apart from his total disinclination for this cocksure fellow's company, meals could be handled differently without Minnie's regulating force.

Una said, 'I'm not coming in now, Dad; I'm not hungry.'

It was a couple of days since Thady had come. He might be gone by the time Minnie returned and then again he might not. Minnie did not like his sudden ways but was biding him for the present; he was someone Jack liked and then he had those scholarly parents. She had met neither but Jack had been to their house in Cork. He could not be drawn to say much about them. Eccentric, some people called them, he said, and that was all. Theirs were names known in educational matters: sometimes they were quoted in the *Educational Monthly*; they wrote articles. Education counted very highly with Minnie. That, to quite a degree, was why she was biding Thady.

Thady sat down by Una's two stones, the book still in his hand. Una had seen him looking at the stones a number of times since his arrival.

'They are good stones,' he said now. 'In fact, they are remarkable.'

'That's why I brought them here.'

'You did? How?'

Tell him the story since Jack apparently had not done so? But no: that picture of Mary Ellen Whelan was not to be dwelt upon again.

'Oh just…' And yet she could have his attention as much as Maggie, only in a different way.

She did not want either to think about Jack and the city cousin and the eiderdown quilt. Certain things too near fear had to get wrapped away inside you until you could find out how to laugh at them the way Thady Keane laughed at everything.

She could have brought Sean to see Maggie going down the roof on her bottom. She could have had revenge for the lies those years before, about the matches, about the wall clock. It was no love for Maggie that stopped her. It was something else, she was not fully sure what. Not to be seen as a telltale by Thady was certainly part of it.

A green storm wracked the glen.

'I love it, I love it,' she shouted, 'I'm mad about the wind!'

The ash trees and hazel bushes were doing a wild dance. One of those warm summer gales. She raced crazily through the rushes, across hummocks. He could barely keep up.

'Here, here,' he yelled over the wind. He grabbed her arm. 'Look at that moss down there in the shelter. We'll take a breather. Come on.'

He dragged her. She could still have broken away. Surprise was the weakener. And something else.

'I could like you for a thing or two but they wouldn't be your looks.'

'You're no beauty yourself, Thady, if paying compliments is the game.'

'It's a good mossy bank. And dry. What about it, Una?'

'No. No again. Don't think I'm like Maggie.'

'Maybe better you were. You think you're a

superior creature to her, don't you?'

'Of course I don't.' Of course he was right. 'And look who's talking—you yourself always acting the know-all, always one up on everyone else. You're quite convinced only your way of thinking is worth anything.'

'You don't know what you're talking about.'

'There you are again.'

'Come on Una, let me show you…'

'No, I said. Jack could come along—we don't know when to expect him back, do we? But besides, that's not the reason.'

If only he were Andrew Rydall. If only he were, what then? Only a few weeks gone since in imagination she was a cloistered ascetic.

When Jack got home, he found Thady reading in the garden between Una's two stones

'Mother of God!' Minnie back from the retreat. Experiencing some fresh impact of horror. Unlike her husband, frequently she found no opportunity to have a quick read of the paper until after the rosary, just before bed. 'Those Reds! Antichrists…God help those poor priests in Mexico…'

'It's not all in the papers either,' Thady said. He had that twist to his mouth that gave you the feeling he was laughing at you. Jack and he were never in for the Rosary. Sometimes they were not in until three or four in the morning. Thick as thieves. It was certainly true that Thady Keane had affected Jack. She didn't know if she liked how. It was difficult really to know what to make of Thady Keane.

Jack was going to whitewash the dugout. Of course it

was no longer just a dugout but the name stuck. Over the years, he had developed it into a sizeable workshed. Weatherproof. The old limekiln near it had been built two generations ago by his grandfather Normile. Sean had never found any use for it; Jack had in plenty. Over the years, also, he had become friendly with Andrew Rydall through their common interest in various things. Andrew described the extended and weatherproofed dugout as 'quite a feat'. Even Thady Keane had praised it—praise indeed. Under the cylindrical cavity of the limekiln, Jack's fire of hard black *caoráin* was hotter, he said, than any English coal.

Sitting on a moss-covered boulder, Una watched and listened. Exclusion of her was in the past.

Thady Keane was the first to spit. A large well-accumulated spit which made a maddened sizzle on the treated lime stones, wearing itself completely out in a few seconds. A whitish limey spot showed on the pink-grey surface where it had expired.

'Ready for the water, they are,' Jack said.

One by one each spat. An unrehearsed ritual. Andrew Rydall laid his bicycle down on the grass path so as to aim. He spat with a special gusto.

'Primitive,' he then said with clear enjoyment.

'Marvellous. You chaps get on with the rest—it's new to me.'

'Jaysus!' exclaimed Tony, he who had been the young apprentice salesman at Neary's. 'I only ever heard of how to make lime.' When his uncle, with whom he had always lived, had bought the Whelan place fairly recently he had moved there with him. Since then he had cycled to work at Neary's every day. But things were changing for him. For them all.

'Take comfort. A first time for everything. Even for

Jack who now knows everything—almost. Right, Jacko?' Always, still, the sardonic twist to Thady's lips. He took the long tongs to half fill one of the buckets with baked stones. They gave off an arc of heat, in passage.

'Hold on now,' Jack put up a hand before beginning to pour river water from the other bucket carefully over the cooked stones. 'Take care for skin, for eyes.' Then in a controlled curve, he poured. There was a hissing, and little webs of vapour which became tendrils vanishing upwards. Then a rapid stirring with a hazel stick, ready cut. They took turns at stirring.

'Jaysus!' Tony exclaimed again, 'Quicklime!'

'Mrs Normile was reading about it in the paper last night. Mexico. They buried a priest to his neck and threw quicklime in his eyes to burn them out of him. We could have used some of that in Tubbernagur, right Jacko? Why didn't we ever think of it?'

'I can think of a few you'd use it on. Yes.'

'And you not? Sudden virtue!'

Banter and not banter. Their school, their victims to their chins. That, Andrew Rydall could understand. Doubtless. Very well. Something else in common. Satan in the guts.

Tony, too. Mental flash of Maurice Neary to his dickie-bow in the ground. And then quicklime as far as the moustache.

Thady went on: 'I told your mother last night it wasn't all in the papers; you can't imagine a newspaper here calling a spade a spade.'

'You're talking about the priest they tied naked to a post and then letting the starving calves loose on him.'

'Jaysus! Those are bad things, bad things. But,'

Tony asserted, 'I'm goin' anyway.'

'Always cruelty. Always that,' Andrew said, 'You're not going for that.'

'I'm goin' for the hell of it, I'd nearly go anywhere to get away from Neary. I'd rather go there than to England or to Boston—there's too many Irish in those places already. I'll take up with a Mexican senorita!'

Jack leant on the hazel stick. 'And I'm going to whitewash what I was going to whitewash—and I'll be struggling with my finals when you're making out with your senoritas.'

Thady pointed at the river. 'You can drown in an inch of that water there if you fall the wrong way. So what? After my finals I'll be heading off, maybe before that. I could fight against the Brits—I speak good German,'—a sly look at Andrew as he said it— 'and then again I could fight against the Gerries. It's all in the game.'

No one spoke bravery or yellow. They would be going their ways for their different reasons. Each had come with individual markings. They had in comm- on youth and the enduring enigma before them.

'Rydall, you'll be going in the missions.'

'I should have thought that would be more likely in your case, Thady—Tubbernagur trains mission- aries, doesn't it?'

A surprise jab. But Andrew's voice indicated malaise: he was verging on that difficult territory of Protestant and Catholic; traditional divergences, injustices, latent or lingering sorenesses best skirted now. He hurried on, 'But I know what you mean— my father and aunt and so on—only they were misfits.'

Thady laughed a grating noise. Then he said, 'Una'll be going in the nuns.'

'No, not I.'

'What will you do, Una?'

'Ah, too soon to know; waiting for results…maybe in a few weeks…'

By evening the whitewashing was done. They had all taken turns. No one would say it was in the nature of any ceremony. To say anything like that would probably evoke a philistine slash from Thady, a glum grunt from Jack. Yet as they stood around, while the sun grew red over the western bog, a silence settled briefly upon them. Perhaps a momentary linked thinking? Phases in their young lives. An end, a beginning. Would they be together in quite this way ever again?

Fifteen

June–July 1942

It was odd that Mrs Riverdale, too, went in for colouring her hair an unlovely orange. The woman surely must never have taken a really straight look at herself. If she had, her hair could not be on show like that. Fooling herself, imagining her head still appeared as did her daughter's, which was indeed a fine curly thick auburn mop. Was it a Protestant female peculiarity, this penchant for dyed orange ageing locks? Elfrida Rydall, too. But Elfrida was someone quite different from Mrs Riverdale: somehow her side curls, seen long ago at the rim of the cloche hat, were likeable. They were not flagrant. They touched you in some way.

Mrs Riverdale asked Una in the burgeoning garden of her home, 'Do you believe in absolute or relative?'

She was stripping a bush of its blackcurrants. Una made no reply for the simple reason that she had no idea what the question meant. But she was not going to reveal that. Nelson had left her alone with this awful woman to help pick the blackcurrants they were to take back with them—part of her loud bounty. The luncheon, too, had been bountiful. Hateful. Una suffered it for the sake of experience.

Around the corner of the house where the Dublin hills rose behind the beech hedge, Nelson was standing beside the vintage car belonging to Mrs Riverdale's son, Oisin. Inside the bowels of the engine, Oisin Riverdale was executing various manipulations while Nelson and a couple of other Trinity men looked on. Unlike his mother and sister, Oisin had no hair whatever, the head thrust under the bonnet of the car being completely bald. It had fascinated Una and repelled her. He could have been younger than Nelson. While saying he was useless with machinery, Nelson had volunteered to hold tools: they also serve who only stand and wait, he said. The other men and Oisin—they were all of the School of Engineering—talked turbines while the repair was being carried out. During luncheon, they had addressed no word to Una. Nor had the lovely daughter who had skipped and hummed her progress from garden bower to table in a strapless sunsuit. A flaming figure with blazing hair.

Throughout the ample meal, deftly served by two uniformed maids, the conversation had rattled over abstract art, the Black Elk Group, the latest play at the Gate, and the impossibility of the Irish language.

'Lovely names—witness Oisin—but an impossible tongue. You can say neither yes nor no in it.' Mrs Riverdale said, at which remark there was protracted laughter from her supporters, of whom Mr Riverdale was not one in this assertion. They congratulated one another that they had never had to learn it.

'Not true. About yes and no. It depends on how you use it.' Una tried to tune into their bright trivial key. Her first offering and it came unnaturally.

'Oh really?' Mrs Riverdale was crushingly light and raced on to the next topic, the garden fruit: 'And here it comes, at its succulent best.' She threw wide her arms in receptivity as the maids brought in dishes of strawberries, jugs of cream, bowls of caster sugar.

Very good food, yes. Sophisticated chatter, yes.

She was not at ease. Not at all. But it was a further stage of learning. She was hungrier for the wider learning which encompassed the strawberries and cream, the manner of serving, what the glut of fruit symbolised of a lifestyle, than for the dish itself. Never before had she seen such largesse of it. How people lived! Mary Ellen Whelan and a hen picking a crumb from the apron on her battered corpse. Dinny Doyle and the smeared, dried residue of food down his front. Maurice Neary and his three precise cups of tea, secret lust for very young girls, in behind the oblong moustache like a grey caterpillar, the dickie-bow, butterfly collar. Proinsias de Burca and his naked house wherein the only edible thing seemed to be a tin of sickly-sweet condensed milk.

Protestants were nicer, she had said to Minnie because of the Rydalls, especially Andrew. She was discovering not all of them were. Mrs Riverdale was a bitch. Her son and daughter had no idea of ordinary courtesy. The Deerings at the train station in Moygrane, putting on no airs whatever, had genuine good manners. Mr Riverdale sat at the head of the table, opposite his wife—could it have been the end, since Mrs Riverdale seemed to initiate all procedures? Una was placed at his left hand. He spoke quietly to her now and then under the non-stop splatter of the others. He asked about her job, if she could manage to follow the course in Trinity she had mentioned and which she so much wished to do. Opposite Nelson sat the daughter with her glowing tresses. Una had always yearned for heavy tresses, any colour. Nelson made no repartee—it was not his usual way—but ate assiduously. Good food he loved. His long thin face. His porridge lunches. His memories of sumptuous tables, his penurious present existence working his way through college, scholarships alone not covering needs. Going his dogged way. Unashamedly relishing anything from the rich man's table.

Mrs Riverdale—fat, dyed, thick wrists, thickening all over, denying her years, wrinkled, powdered—flirted with the Trinity men, her son included. She had her eye on Nelson. For her daughter. His lack of money would not matter: the Riverdales had plenty. His background was the thing. That air he carried. Quiet. Indications of interesting private territories. Women liked Nelson.

Sixteen

Were a person to do it at all a person would become one of these—a carer of lepers, of the mad, a Carmelite?

In the end she had chosen none of them.

I am not of the stuff.

I am not of the stuff. Too greedy. Too fierce an appetite for living—so many other kinds of living which there must be.

It had taken many tramps around the land. Much thinking, hidden in coppices by the river.

Not the stuff to go that way. University. Yes. Yes. But impossible. Jack had to be the one. I can see that. Don't grudge him. Can take it. Was glad to boast about his medical course to the others in Marymount. What use is our county council? Other county councils in the province award scholarships. If only I'd been Jack. If only there were more money to come by. Jack doesn't value his luck.

Jack had not got all his exams first time. Such failures threw Minnie and Sean into states of extreme distress. Feelings in the house became highly charged and exploded in vilification of him and agonised exhortation. Una despised Jack's bit measures: he should have aimed high, taking pride in doing so. Jack, with the privilege of University, seemed to find almost a hangdog pleasure in a mediocre record. The hurt pride of his parents in front of enquiring neighbours and townspeople did not seem to affect him. And yet he continued to thrive in the home country, exploring further the kinds of things he had always been drawn to: his wayward experiments, endless arbitrary reading, the fashioning of this and that unexpected object, his drawing. While still at Tubbernagur, the one thing that had delighted him was the extra access to French which Father Twomey had made possible. He had done well, gaining prizes from French educational bodies. If he could have transposed himself, along with all he cared about in Balnahown, to some part of France, he probably would have been as near content as he would ever be. Minnie and Sean, of course, held unshakably that his safest line to the future was becoming a doctor. The tension in regard to him was sustained by the opposing forces of their heartbreaking anxiety for his good and his seeming indifference to it.

None of his reading in the holidays had to do with his course work. He talked of Heidegger, nihilism, Marx. He needled Una wih a prick of his earlier mockery.

'For all your high doings in Marymount, you know nothing of them. You badly need to catch up.'

'Oh, I'll catch up, no fear. I'll read Marx or anyone else because I want to. It's easy to keep up with you, Jack. No bother.'

Some of her strengths were much stronger than his now. And that was sad, too. Things had changed between them. Still deeply caring for him, she had moved out of her younger tormented adoration of him which, when so constantly rejected, took self-defeating forms. She had long moved away from longing for his approval.

'And now, Una, with the Leaving Cert well and truly out of the way, what will you do with your two choices?'

'Well, Mam, I won't go on for teacher training. I'd end up here, wouldn't I? A country school. No slur on all your hard work, Mam—but…I want to get out. Out and away. See all sorts of things. See… everything.'

'So? Well, all there is, is the civil service.'

'I know, and I'll take it; it's there waiting. Not that it will be…everything. But it'll be a start. I'll be earning. Bit by bit I'll be finding out about living in the capital. I'll have to see how I fit in with the civil service. Once in Dublin, there are bound to be…ways. I want to see about the university. Want to…expand. See and see, do and do…'

'Easy, Una, take it easy now. You'll stay at Mrs. Breen's of course. Jack will be there to help.'

'OK about Mrs Breen's but whenever did Jack help? Help me, especially? So what will I be needing him for, anyway?'

'Well, he'll maybe settle you in.'

'Fat lot! If he were like Andrew Rydall, now, I'd believe it.'

'Anyway, we'll tell him to show you where to go the first day.'

And Jack did meet her at Kingsbridge Station. Dark and grimy, so much so, it could have oppressed her. But this night it signified the threshold of independence. Of endless dicovery. However sombre and gloomy, the place was exciting.

The girl with him Jack introduced as Hannah. 'It's

Thady's sister.'

Why had he never mentioned her before? Keep your surprise to yourself.

Jack looked thinner. Strained. Never before had she seen him with a girl. She had wondered sometimes at his having no apparent urge to go to the dance halls, the obvious places of selection down at home. All their younger life, references to females from him tended to come as denigration. At Balnahown through the years, his interests seemed to be constant, the old interests—with the addition in more recent times of drink. Time and again the smell of it hung around him since his days at University College. Sean and Minnie tackled him on it every so often. They both had a horror of it. The uncle in the States, Sean's older brother and sender of the unedifying blue pictures, had killed himself with booze there. The bad drop in the blood and pubs were both anathema, unceasingly to be guarded against. Sean had had to take 'the pledge' before Minnie would agree to marry him.

The smell was off Jack tonight.

What to say to a girl, totally unexpected, accompanying him on this new terrain? Maybe her presence meant Thady's also, somewhere near? By way of trying to cover her surprise, she asked, 'Is Thady up, too, then?'

'Ah no,' the girl said. 'Sure Thady is in Cork all the time—hasn't he still his finals to finish?'

This utterance made Una no wiser. Neither Jack nor Hannah offered any further enlightenment.

'You're working here, are you Hannah?'

She was blackhaired like Thady and once you knew they were brother and sister you could see the resemblances. But Hannah did not wear glasses; her

164

eyes were large, quick.

'Yes, I am. Didn't Jack ever tell you?' An aggrieved note there? 'I'm a nurse at the hospital.'

The implied assumption that Una should have known about her gave just a little more light on the matter.

'I see. Well…I'm glad to have people meeting me off the train.'

She would have preferred Jack on his own. Hannah's being there did not make him any more accessible than usual. Indeed, he seemed unforthcoming in a new way. He took her suitcase, saying, 'Mrs Breen's is near enough for us to walk. There's no direct bus anyway and taxis are beyond the beyond. We'll take the shortcut up here.'

They went up a lane which took them past St James's Hospital.

'That's not where I work, though,' Hannah volunteered.

There came wafting a curious smell on the night air. Una asked them, 'What is it? Is it from the hospital?'

'Tis the brewery. Hops. Guinness's.' Jack was gruff. ''Tis just down there.' He gestured to his left.

'Ah, chilt!' Mrs Breen welcomed her. Her father's once frequent word for her, sounding so different in Mrs Breen's strong accent. She was Dutch. It was their first meeting. The agreement was that she would share Mrs Breen's bedroom, there being no other space available. Minnie had said, 'Ah sure you'll be all right. She's charging only twenty-five shillings a week for board and keep. You can't afford more out of your start-off salary. Maybe in a while you can change if you want to, when your pay goes up a bit. Anyway, sure it's good to be where Jack is.'

Una had not been too sure about that. Only time would tell.

Jack put her case down in the heterogeneously cluttered space that was Mrs Breen's bedroom.

'I'll leave you to it now,' he said. 'I'm seeing Hannah to the bus. I'll take you to that civil service place tomorrow—in the morning.'

'That girl,' Mrs Breen commented when they had gone, 'isn't looking so goot these days.'

The remark implied familiarity with Hannah. Una had no answer. The notion of Hannah as an acknowledged feature of Jack's life in Dublin was something to get used to.

The next morning, true to his promise, Jack took her to the building in O'Connell Street where she got her briefing for work. Jack looking after her. That in itself was a new experience. She would not tax him; he could tire very rapidly of being her guide around town.

'She's fat,' Jack had said in Balnahown, a year after he had begun his lodger's tenure in Mrs Breen's. 'She's fat from eating big feeds when we are all out.'

His antipathies had extended from Tubbernagur and other abhorred targets to include aspects of Dublin and people in his ambit there. He raked up the oddities and weak points of Mrs Breen with sour joy. About his landlady's alleged big feeds, Minnie had laughed, and then she countered, 'How do you know that—that she lashes into food when you re out?'

She defended Mrs Breen. On brief visits to Dublin, she had stayed at the digs. She had not faulted them. They suited the only outlay she and Sean could make for Jack's bed and board.

'I can tell. She skimps us and gorges herself.'

'I don't believe it. Anyway, I'd say more power to the wretched woman. Look at all she has to do on her own—what use to her is that man of hers?'

True, Pat Breen could be seen as more of a burden than otherwise. Once a seaman, he had been left deaf and lame by an accident on the trawler plying to Rotterdam. He heard more, was capable of more than he cared to admit; this was Minnie's view. In any case, it would appear he used his disabilities to madden his wife. Requiring him to do some small repair—for he was quite a handyman—or go on some errand and to save herself the stairs, his wife would scream from the hall at him where he holed up securely in the return room. She had once thought the world of him in his naval cap—there was a photo of him, thus, on the piano, handsome with his excellent teeth used in a knowing smile: he knew he could readily have her from her Dutch home where her mother ran rooms for seamen. And so she came to Dublin a lifetime ago, and to the hard times after his accident while he was still in his early forties. His compensatory pension was not enough for the education of their one child, who had music in her which ought to be developed. So Mrs Breen took lodgers as her mother had done in Rotterdam. Her English she had learned through daily necessity, having a usage which was a bullseye for Jack's ridicule. Minnie delighted in the awkward but expressive phraseology, prizing the errors where she would have scathed her pupils.

'There are four lodgers, Jack; she does all the cleaning,' Minnie said, 'the shopping, the meals three times a day, looking after his nibs as well—and would you grudge her a bite on her own when the house might be quiet? Do you ever think of that, Jack?'

Jack did not, of course. Jack nor Sean nor any man to be come across in the home district would ever consider the energy expended in the tasks of women. The one exception was the shoemaker in Poulanara to whose bench the shoes of the Normile family were taken for repair. His bench was just inside the window, in a section of the kitchen partitioned off, clearly visible from the street; his wife did dressmaking in a tiny back room. Between them they took turns at running the house for their five children. Instead of commending the cobbler for his domesticated proclivities, Minnie's verdict on him, contrarily, was that he was a bit of a molly.

Seventeen

A notable forehead. Above it, the hair was thick, careless. He was a large angular presence, the man Penn Reade to whom Nelson gave allegiance of a special character, whose views did not please so many, amongst them Nelson's people. Without those views it was unlikely the meeting of Nelson Forterre with Una Normile would have occurred.

Beatrice Reade was a quiet person. People, at first, tended to be deceived by her mild manner. At first, they might consider her submissive to his forceful way. In reality she had a mind of her own with ideas sometimes strongly divergent from his. But in company, she avoided contradicting him. Her avoidance arose from loyalty. There were always plenty of others ready to query, counter, tear apart, sift, abuse. She would leave them the floor; things needed to be thrashed out. In private she would state her case.

The broth she made for the Friday circle from marrowbones and vegetables was lacking in taste for two reasons—the Emergency (the name given in Ireland to wartime conditions), and her lack of interest in cooking. People partook of the soup sitting where they could—the room was always full. Several sat on the floor. A number of the men wore corduroy trousers, bright woollen socks and sandals. There was one with hair in a Lisztean sweep, one with perfume. Amongst the women were two eye-catchers

169

for opposite reasons: the dowd—was this what was known as bluestocking? wondered Una; the exquisite whom wartime clothes rationing seemed not to affect—silk suit, gossamer stockings, kid shoes. She did not sit on the floor; her lovely legs, disposed in the most decorative arrangement, were a distraction. Both men and women, Penn Reade excepted, could lose the thread of discourse should their eyes chance on a view of them. The owner of these attractions was introduced to Una as Gladys Peach-Orr. Madeline, the Reade daughter, later said in Una's hearing, 'Gladys Peach-Orr is a pain in the neck.'

Madeline Reade did not attend the Friday circle and made an appearance only to help her mother dispense the soup. Her father well knew of her antipathy to Gladys Peach-Orr. To the Friday gathering he upheld the desirability of universal love while seeking to handle the reality of its non-existence. Speaking to Madeline inside the limits of the family, he said it was a pity her attitude was so often virulent. Doubtless, he said, he was not without blame regarding her. What parent, no matter how earnest, is blameless. Without a doubt, he had made mistakes. To explore new thinking in matters of child upbringing was not to be proof against inadvertent error in practice. The persistent operation of error in human behaviour, no matter how sincere, had to be acknowledged and, ideally, forgiven. A sense of humour was invaluable.

Nelson had said to Una, 'Penn Reade, you'll find, emphasises freedom of thinking, looking in—at everything there—freedom of speech. No censorship. Strong, too, on forgiving. To really forgive, really do it, is probably one of the very hardest things.'

Una had come in quickly, 'Nothing new, that. We sang it off in catechism class: Forgive your enemies, says Christ, do good to them that hate you, pray for them that curse you—I was about ten, maybe. And then, isn't it Pope who says, "To err is human, to forgive, divine"?'

'Nothing new at all,' he had agreed, 'but we don't, do we?'

'Now, no censorship, that's new to me. I was brought up on censorship.'

Madeline, having her father's fluency and none of her mother's forbearance, freely gave her opinion of the Friday circle. Her father surrounded himself with nut-cases, self-absorbed. tearing, as it were, their mental and emotional entrails out, peering and poking at the stinking things, imagining that by these activities they were going to reshape the world. This public putrescence she wanted no part of. She vented these convictions only in family privacy—that allowed for the presence of a few, very close intimates of whom Nelson Forterre was one.

Her father said, 'You have never interested yourself enough, Madeline, stayed long enough, to know what really is at work. All right—ready ground for a laugh, and you amuse. And you are entitled to your opinions. But not everything should be trivialised. You give a very distorted version.'

Mildly, her mother remarked, 'You have much to learn, Madeline.'

Una did not like the soup. It was thin and lacking in flavour. The war, I suppose, she thought. Yet in Balnahown, war or no war, soup was always a rich texture; afterwards you remembered the taste. Even in Marymount, excellent soups had been prepared for the exam progamme in cookery classes, if not for the daily menu. She did like Beatrice Reade herself.

Gladys Peach-Orr, unlike Mrs Riverdale, seemed to be someone naturally gracious. Undulating winningly towards Una, she invited her to go blackberrying one autumn afternoon should the weather be kind. Charmingly. She had, she said, a little blue car. The activity proposed was not one with which Una could readily associate Gladys, who did not at all resemble the sort of person—Una herself, for example—to suffer cheerfully scratches, pricks, and smears for the sake of obtaining wild fruit. She seemed a creature born to *couture*, and the availability of service.

'Raymond,' Gladys said, 'will come too.' She touched the shoulder of the man who sat on the floor near her knees. 'Raymond, this is Una, Nelson's friend.'

'They are lovers,' Nelson said afterwards. 'Gladys is divorced. She is constant in her change of lovers.'

The time Gladys had suggested was still some months away, allowing plenty of space for the proposal to be forgivably forgotten but the invitation was disarming. More, it was warming. Subtantiating winningness, she added, 'But before that, you must come to dinner, You and Nelson—soon, Nelson?'

'We would like to very much, wouldn't we, Una?'

'Yes. Thank you.'

'Wednesday a good night for you?'

Nelson consulted the little diary he always carried in his pocket— many strands to keep track of: part-time office, research for newspaper articles, theatre nights for review, studies, social events, Una.

'Well, Wednesday a fortnight would be better if that suits you, too, and if you don't mind our leaving a bit early—a work commitment later. I can't afford to turn down work. And thanks, Gladys.'

At the door Beatrice Reade stood with her husband.

'We are glad to have met you, Una.' Her manner was simple, her tone natural. 'We would like you and Nelson to come to supper some time soon. Could you both manage it?'

'Very kind, thank you.' The diary came out again, an evening was arranged.

February 1942

Squash them with your molars. Roll the squash around inside your mouth. The absolute indulgence. One after the other. And no conscience. A half-crown's worth out of my very first wages. Greedy and no guilt. I've a right, haven't I?

A special day. Even a bit of sun today. Promise of spring. English people say it doesn't begin until the twenty-first of March. I prefer it our way, Saint Bridget's Day. Soon maybe I could sit without a coat to watch the water fowl. Wishful thinking. Away too soon yet for that. Although you could say there is a special energy, a spring energy in those ducks today, flurrying in all directions. Pity that girl coming up now has to look so sad. Dark head dropped low. Eyes on the ground instead of on the water birds and all that terrific paddling. But it's...

'Hannah! Hello, Hannah.'

'Una!' The sad face under the black hair. A very slight smile. Guarded look.

'You'd very nearly passed me by—I didn't

recognise you.'

'I didn't recognise you, either.'

It was their second meeting. In the fortnight intervening since her arrival at Kingsbridge Station, Una had had only a few glimpses of Hannah as she went out of sight somewhere or other with Jack. She had not called to the digs since.

'I've just got into my hand my first ever earned money. All of five pounds. A fortnight's earnings. Just three-quarters of an hour ago.'

'God, aren't you the wealthy one!'

She was Thady Keane's sister, no doubt. The twist of her mouth at that moment could have been his.

'Well, it *is* wealth to me. Half of it I've put aside to give to Mrs Breen. That left two ten for myself—till the next pay.'

'So you bought yourself a bag of something.'

Hannah stood over her, the half-smile mocking.

'I did indeed. Have one. Aren't you going to sit? Rich dark chocolates. I was told Noblett's was good for chocolates so I brought my ration book and bought half-a-crown's worth.'

'And now you're having a real greedy time. I bet you're sorry you called me over.'

'I'll have to admit to it, the greed. I'm the greediest thing.' Only so short a time ago—it seemed ages now—she, Una Normile—had seriously envisaged herself an adherent of the ascetic life. 'I had to have a splurge with my first money. And so I came here to Stephen's Green to gorge. Go on, have one.'

Hannah made a grimace.

'To tell you the truth, I don't want any. But thanks. I appreciate the big effort you're making there. Oh, they're very rich looking.'

She turned away in distaste at the sight of the

glossily dark confections. She sat very straight on the edge of the park seat.

'I bought a dress-length too…'

'Great!' There was no lift to it, however.

'Not for myself. It's my Mam's birthday soon. I posted it off in Anne Street, *before*, now notice *before* I bought the sweets.'

'God you're a good girl altogether.' A pause. 'And how's Jack today?'

'I don't see much of Jack. I didn't see him this morning before I left for work. You're likely to see more of him…but since you ask, it strikes me that, when I do see him, Jack isn't in such good form.'

Hannah got up abruptly. 'I'll be late for my shift. I'm to be on duty. I'll see you—maybe, and maybe I won't.' Thady's sister all right.

'Maybe. I must get back to the office myself.'

They took different directions.

Buying that material for Mam and posting it off, buying and eating those chocolates, those two things gave me immense pleasure.

Minnie had not faulted the digs because not faulting them was expedient.

In reality, it was a dreary house. You entered a dark hallway with its lodging house aura of shut doors and trapped air. A few nondescript coats drooped on a stand. In the dead of winter the place could be depressing.

Una was not to be depressed. Life was opening out; her zest for it leapt the days. Spring was on the way. But Jack complained. He continued to look strained. Too thin. Sometimes his sister thought he even looked unhealthy. In Balnahown he tramped miles over the land to good fishing. In Dublin he took no exercise nor did he join in any sports at the university. When he wasn't in the library, he crouched over books in the room he shared with another lodger, Seamus.

The front room, Jack told Una who had never seen it, for it had been sealed ground ever since her arrival, was full of calamitous furniture and brass things. The week prior to her coming, it had been opened up and a real fire kept going there, a few nights before Mrs Breen's daughter got married. Jack and the other lodgers got invited to join a few neighbours, and friends of the couple. They filled the place. He did not like gatherings like that but stayed a while because of the fire and sandwiches. No further such warming event was likely to occur for the rest of the winter in the house. When again would there be a good fire and the chance of a bit of extra food in the night?

Una believed Jack suffered even more from the cold than she had done in Marymount. A dank chill pervaded the digs. For a few hours each evening a strip of dull red showed under a peevish bank of slack in the room called the dining room, in which, however, no one ever dined. The lodgers were free to sit here should they wish. The kitchen, where meals were eaten, had no heating other than that generated by the gas stove while cooking was in progress. The Emergency, the Emergency! Mrs Breen repeatedly bemoaned.

And it was. The war, as the world knew it. Una kept trying to follow the war reports. It was very difficult. She set out to ask Jack about them, news-paper in hand. Seamus was out; he'd be alone in the room. Seamus, Jack had told her, put his glass eye in a mug of water every night. To soak. The two of them were on good terms, seeming not to be on top of each other, not overly afflicted by incidental annoyances. Or if these existed, they must have been cancelled out by the unfailing good humour of Seamus. There was also the fact that Jack, so protective at home of his territory, had nothing at all with him in this lodging house bedroom that he considered precious. Everything precious was in Balnahown. The textbooks that lay about him were necessary just now, valued only for his course, to be sold off when he was finished with them.

She knocked on his door, getting a mumble in answer. He seemed always so low in energy. Should she not feel sorry for him that he could not enjoy the discovery of new things all the time, as she did? She did not feel sorry. She was impatient with his slant to diminish continually the life about him, railing at lecturers, Dublin shoneens, coursework, the digs, Mrs Breen, the fourth lodger whom he christened Yak-yak. Was he missing Thady Keane? He seemed to have no comparable companion in Dublin. Could that be why he had taken up with Thady's sister? If so, then he seemed no happier as a result. And Hannah herself? She had moved away suddenly the other day, having just asked about Jack.

When she came into his room, she found him slouched over a large tome and a notebook, a blanket pulled off his bed around his shoulders.

'Working hard?'

'I hate the stuff.'

'Your exam soon now?'

'I'll go down in it.'

'What makes you say that?'

'Those fuckers have it in for me. Never give me a fair chance.'

'Rotten if it's true, but is it?'

'What else? I know the stuff. I know it well. They're just down on me. I'm freezing. Had to stay up here—Yak-yak is in the other freeze-hole.' Dining room. 'Never stops.'

'You should have stayed in the library.'

'I got hungry, God's sake. Came back here for my dinner. Can't afford food out.'

'I've brought the paper—came to ask you about the war.'

'Don't. Fucking war. Madness. Why don't we go to the pictures? *Dodge City* is on at the Nova down the road. We'll be warm at least.'

'What about Hannah?'

'What about her?'

'I mean shouldn't she be going to *Dodge City* with you?'

'Should she? She's busy. Isn't she?'

'I don't know. Just asking.'

He said no more. Seamus came in. His news was, it turned out, his girlfriend was unexpectedly working overtime. They were saving to get married; overtime was not to be sneezed at. Seamus, with his glass eye and job in a shoe factory, was able to find fun in so many things. Turned things to fun most of the time. Especially the factory floor. Una did not want Jack-the-joker but it did cloud matters that Jack always seemed so out of gear. Despite the dreariness of the digs, the penetrating chills—and they were easing away a bit latterly—and difficulties with studies, Jack had so much that Seamus never had:

education all the way up, a home to return to, Minnie and Sean, decent parents. Seamus was an orphan, product of an institute.

'We're going to the pictures, Seamus, do you want to come with us?'

'Sure an' I will so, Jack. No harm done. Sure it's only one and threepence. Have a laugh.'

And so they went.

'It could be managed. Sometimes the place is deserted. In the dead of night no one seems over-conscientious about doing rounds. You know how it is yourself. You know that, you've done your night stints.'

'It depends on the sister on duty.'

'That Sister Carroll takes things easy. There are the long cups of tea in the kitchen. It could be managed. We could use one of the small labs off the corridor. Blinds down, black-out.'

'Jack it...frightens me.'

'You could plead sick for a couple of days after.'

'I could do that but...it's what you'd have to do I'm most worried about. Do you feel able? Do you feel sure about what you have to do? Would I...would I be made a mess of?'

'You won't be.'

'Jesus! I could maybe...die...don't you care? You're so cold-blooded about it all.'

'I'm not. Not one bit. But what other way is there? We've gone into it all. Marrying is out.'

'It really is, is it? Is it?'

'You know it is, Hannah. Altogether. For the last time I'll say it. We've been through all that. We've been through everything. England—all that. I'll

179

probably never be the marrying kind.'

'I'm inclined to believe it.'

'Well then…'

'Jesus, I'm frightened! You will know how to go about it? You've failed some exams.'

'I've failed out of lack of interest in certain aspects. Nothing in this line. Hannah be quiet now. I do know—I've always been sure in that line of work.'

Eighteen

June–July 1942

Penn Reade drank from the jug placed near the cups. Beatrice Reade rose and fetched a glass. Into this she poured milk for her husband, then took away the jug from which he had drunk and brought another instead. These things she did unobtrusively. While he ate—as if he had starved for days—Penn Reade talked. It was Madeline who cut across whatever her father was saying, pointedly underlining the milk-drinking from the jug incident, which had been somehow given a kind of awry acceptability—part of the man—by her mother's quiet procedure.

'I could have done that, Mummy.' Madeline was clear, incisive while giving her father a certain look. Her mother made no reply but, having sat down, continued to eat unhurriedly.

The meal proceeded, Nelson and Una the only guests. At the table were also two cousins, students, who had lived as part of the family since both their parents died. They and Nelson challenged Penn Reade at points. Talk did not cease a minute.

'Go easy on the butter, Nelson.' Madeline called from across the large round table. Banter, but delivered with the brusquerie of one determined to establish a practical note to counter the prevailingly conceptual discourse. The inference was plain: her father talked too much, and irrelevantly to the demands of common sense. 'Clergymen in the making may not be rationed in Trinity but everyone

181

out here is.'

'Madeline!' the cousins expostulated.

Nelson looked her in the eye. 'Watch it, Madeline,' he said easily, 'you are upsetting your cousins.'

'Don't try for sympathy, Nelson.' The sallies, it would seem, were to engage attention away from her father.

When she married Giles, there would be none of these radical wafflings in her home. Thank heaven for Giles's predictable phlegmatic temperament.

Her dress carried no frill nor adornment, Her blonde hair displayed no frivolous curls. Her plan for the future excluded untidy thinking—these psychological postulations. Her father unnecessarily complicated existence with hypotheses and speculations, attaching inadmissable significance to ordinary everyday acts, positing disguises, accounting for aberrations of conduct with unlikely and sentimental interpretations, dredging up impossible motives of jealousy and violence, insisting embarrassingly on the function of sexuality, even, unthinkably, infant sexuality—all of which matters were best left unmentioned. The family she was marrying into were happily free of such introverted mining and tunnelling. The implementing of a certain number of sensible rules ensured proper behaviour. She and Giles would exemplify that in their children. Giles's father would not dream of drinking from the milk jug. Poor Mummy. Poor, poor bovine Mummy. She needed a thorough shake. Actually what she needed was a...bloody...oh one must not...but that's what springs from an upbringing of free thought...too free...it affects you in spite of yourself, the mind becomes loose, undisciplined. Madeline found it necessary to bring every strongest reaction against him, her father.

'You'll find the Divinity School won't approve, Nelson, of your having had anything to do with me. An obscenity, an excrescence—that is how they see me. Your connection with me will brand you a subversive element. Distinctly harmful to orthodoxy.'

May 1942

The less accessible, serious ones at the *Craobh*, sometimes even hermetic behind their cloaks of pondering, frequently conferred aside. There came from them on occasion emanations of mighty gloomy matter hanging fire, and this was not to everyone's taste. One pale anguished young man shouted on a certain night at the premises, 'Blood must flow again!'

He shouted it over and over, the words pushing out on the breath of drink. Una and her friends did not like it.

When they and she were together at the *Craobh*, they laughed a lot. They were there for the love of the language, for companionship, not for the letting of blood. Once in Dublin, she had quickly searched out girls from Marymount already there. Linking up again with them meant meeting further people, meant joining *Craobh an Dóchais*. They were cheerful, glad of wages newly theirs, happy not to be taking any longer from hard-pressed parents. They were hopeful: *Craobh an Dóchais*—Branch of Hope, they said brightly, appropriate for them. They were full of bright young hope. They had all loved the language, they would continue in their devotion.

At least one night during the week they met at the club, and, at the weekends as the weather became more springlike they cycled up to the hills. They faithfully attended the little club rallies sometimes held at points in the city. From a portable stand, a number of them would speak on a topic, the language cause being the chief one. The pale taut young man who within the the club premises urged the flowing of blood, had spoken a number of times. He had a fine high brow and long fingers. You could imagine him, they said to one another, in a Hollywood film catching the eye in evening clothes, maybe playing the piano to a captivated audience. Then they laughed more: they were crazy, they told themselves, to be talking that way about him for wasn't he a saturated Irish specimen!

Attention to the little gatherings at Mansfield's corner, from passers-by, was unremarkable. However, they carried on: young—the greater number of them, energetic, ebullient and, most often, ready for laughter. Una and her especial pals were amongst the lighter-hearted. Their role as resurrectors and sustainers of the language did not sit grimly on them. Gaiety did not prevent due awareness of the sad aspects of Pearse, one of their heroes, nor frequent reference to his poetry, to that of MacDonagh, to the worthiness of all the martyrs of 1916. The nobility of these had been a constant focus in schooldays, their images enshrined therein. They had been an inspiration. Because of them the country—six counties apart—was a republic, self-governing. *Éire saor, Éire Gaelach*—these new young people were upholding the heroes of 1916 in putting the ancient tongue to the fore; to do so was edifying, it was also fun, part of the enjoyment of being out in the world of Dublin, earning a living.

Una and her friends did not like it when the

serious members conferred aside, giving off dour noises of threat and storm. But they kept together in their enthusiasm for the spoken tongue, for what that gave them of a centre, comradeship, music, dancing, joy. In their workplaces, when they tried to put into practice their principles of always talking Irish, they met in the main with ribaldry.

Jack, of course, mocked. Languages he liked. In Tubbernagur days, he had won prizes for French— several, and Irish—an odd time. In Balnahown, he used go around visiting the scattered few old people still left, for whom Irish had been their first tongue, listening to, and later recounting what they said. He had scored in English. The bits of German he had picked up from Thady Keane, he liked relating to the three languages he knew. In the early hours of the morning, he tuned into wave lengths emitting what he said was Moroccan Spanish. He said the Moorish sounds coming across were like Irish folk songs. His mockery of Una's campaigning was a contradiction of his enjoyment in expression, his entrenched Irishness. But it mattered not at all to her what he said; she saw his attitude to zeal for Irish as a reflection of his fear of self-exposure. Endeavours like hers focused attention on you; his whole instinct was towards seclusion, turning away from gatherings, socialising, towns, cities. It was why he always seemed happiest moving at his own pace through his experimenting and devising in Balnahown. His dugout was of far greater importance to him than the aula maxima.

And what about Hannah?

'I haven't seen any trace of Hannah for ages. Was wondering if she'd like to come to a céilí...'

'Hannah is a free agent.'

'I know you would never come with her.'

'You know right.'

'Well maybe you'd ask her from me?'

'If I see her. If I remember—not likely.'

Like trying to get blood out of a turnip. Still, mixing metaphors, you could read between the lines.

A couple of girls from the *Craobh* waved goodbye to Una. It was near the end of the lunch break. The crusts from their sandwiches were a brief centre of rivalry amongst the ducks; laughing at the antics, the friends went their ways towards different offices. There was still time, Una saw, for a closer look at the bed of spring flowers on the far side of the pond. As she came nearer it, she saw Hannah standing by the flowers, looking at her. Waiting for her, in fact.

'Well Hannah, this seems to be the place to find you. I was talking to Jack about you, only just last night.'

'Were you?'

She looked so pale. Was it the strong light? Or the very black hair that made her look that way?

'It was about a céilí.'

'A céilí?' Astonishment, and something of scorn as well.

'I was saying I hadn't seen you for ages. I was wondering if you'd like to come? They're great sometimes. Of course, Jack didn't want to come.'

'Of course.' Dry.

'And you?'

'Ah…I don't think so…I'm not in the mood.'

'How are you getting on at the hospital?'

'Oh…all right. Only I'm giving up the nursing.'

'You are? That's very sudden.'

'Not really. From the start I wasn't sure whether I'd like it. I'm sure now.'

'Jack never said a word about it. And what will you do?'

'I've been accepted for the uni—UCD. I'll do an Arts degree. I've decided.'

'Well that's good. Isn't Jack pleased? Wonder why he never said.'

'I wonder.'

'Thady will be pleased.'

'Can you imagine Thady saying he's pleased? Much too straightforward for Thady. I'd say he will be, in a...distorted sort of a way. My parents are pleased though. I've hopes of the scholarship.'

'That's what comes of being from County Cork. I'd love to be you. I've longed to go to uni. Have tried for night classes but no go. My parents couldn't manage it—I mean I thought to keep on with my job and so pay for a night course.'

'But you'd get the scholarship...'

'Didn't you know our county doesn't give one? Lucky, lucky you. But I must get back to work.'

'Ah I've just remembered...you were asking me to a céilí but I've something here that you might like—a literary get-together...' She took a typewritten slip from her bag.

'Oh I would, I'm sure I would.'

'I know a few in the UCD English Lit Society and they've organised this get-together with the corresponding lit group in Trinity. It's to be in the Pine Forest. The tearoom there is booked for it. Maybe you'd like to come.'

'Yes, I would, indeed I would...but it depends on the day. I do a lot with *Craobh an Dóchais*. I was hoping to recruit you.'

'No go there, I'm not that sort. Anyway there's the date on this slip. We're to meet at Lincoln Gate on the Saturday morning as you see there. Then we'll cycle up to the Pine Forest. A few weeks yet. Keep the slip.'

'Right. I'll say yes. Another different sort of event. I'm all for new events. I'll do a few extra things with the *Craobh* to make up.'

Neither of them mentioned Jack again.

The term was finished. Jack side-stepped when she asked why he had not mentioned Hannah's change of plan. He affected no interest when she told him of her meeting with Hannah, of Hannah's new plans, of the proposed outing to the Pine Forest.

'A chap from UCD, some northerner, organised it all.'

'I wouldn't want anything of such a caper.' Hannah was welcome to the northerner, whoever he was et cetera. What he wanted was to get back to Balnahown fast. He threw in that he'd most likely gone down in the finals and would have to be back in the autumn for some repeats.

His sister's pity was almost all for Minnie and Sean: they would be devastated by this latest let-down, not least because of the loss of face, yet again, before the whole district and the townspeople. How good it would have been, the uplift of Jack's success.

Nineteen

May 1942

In May came the Saturday morning when, for the first time, she was not meeting the friends from *Craobh an Dóchais*. Instead she was to go with the groups Hannah had spoken about. In the small gathering outside Lincoln Gate she knew no one except Hannah, whose wave of recognition, restrained though it was, she was glad of. Hannah was propped against her bicycle. Beside her was a young man.

'This is the man from the North,' she said, introducing Una to him. A figure, it soon was evident, amongst the students from UCD. A very direct look, a drollery somewhere behind it.

'Not all of us are here yet,' he said. 'We'll wait another wee bit.'

The Trinity people did not object. 'Ours are lazy too,' one of them said. 'Let's wait five minutes more—just.'

Sallies, repartee, jerky laughter—all were kept up to defy awkwardness and unfamiliarity. The proclaimed object of the occasion was a mingling, a bringing of people together from the two seats of learning which, thus far, had functioned too much apart, often in suspicion, auras of superiority, inferiority, in rivalry, various snobberies, backbiting. To mark common ground there were to be humorous literary contributions of a leftist flavour. Tea would happen somewhere in all this. Una heard the accent

189

predominating amongst the Trinity people as the Rydall one.

While they all cycled off through the streets towards Rathfarnham and thence the hills, mingling was not yet possible in the traffic. However, once clear of the city, tentative efforts strengthened; there was interweaving, pairing.

'Hello there, I'm Nelson Forterre.'

'I'm Una Normile.'

'What are you going for in UCD?'

'I'm not there at all.' How she wished she were. 'The civil service is what I'm in. And you, what are you doing?'

'At present thinking of switching—when finished with English and French. Thinking of moving into Divinity. A late decision. I'm a late student. A very late student.'

'What does that mean, divinity? Where does it lead you?'

'It means the Church. Being a clergyman. It's in my family. But tell me about you. What's the civil service like?'

'Very dull.' This was not at all a Balnahown expression, nor a Marymount one either. It was a Rydall one. As it slipped out, she realised that. Andrew had complained his school was very dull. Elfrida would exclaim: 'How dull! No more raspberry jam left.' Una Normile was resorting to a Rydall touch in this unfamiliar context. Why should she do this? But it had happened spontaneously— and the word did describe the civil service. Then why had she not said 'boring', her usual word for it? 'Oh it's all adding up long columns of figures for which I have no head. I really wanted to go to university— that is, go to night classes while keeping the job to pay my way. But there are no night classes.'

'Too bad. Maybe something could be done.' He seemed serious, not just throwing this off, a gambit, as he put effort into cycling the slope.

'What does that mean? What could be done?'

The rise got steeper. They dismounted and pushed the bicycles.

'Well, it's not impossible to fit in the odd lecture— I'm sure the civil service would let you out for that. You don't have to go to all lectures, you know. The rest—of the material—you could study up on your own—with a bit of advice. Why don't you try for Trinity?'

He didn't say Trinity was better, nicer. The outing was to promote good feeling.

Nelson Forterre it was, who chaired the meeting in the Pine Forest tearoom. He liked doing a little with the Trinity group, he had told Una. Not a lot— there wasn't time. For a while he smoked a pipe, having first asked if anyone minded. The whole affair was very informal. They sat around a circle of small tables. The man from the North was the first to speak. What was going on made Una all the more wishful to get into their kind of university life. The talk stimulated. Topics like these were never part of the office. In the office were the tedious columns of figures; the boss on a Monday morning reeking of sour beer and onions; plenty chat about hard (boozed-up) nights; comparisons of nail varnish and lipsticks.

It was surprising how much Hannah had to say. Plain enough she had read plenty. Like Thady, again. The man from the North talked very well: persuasive, sticking to his points, but softly. As there was a general movement out of the room, Hannah held back to turn to Una. 'Say hello to Jack for me.'

'But he's gone to Balnahown already.'

For an instant a flicker of change over Hannah's face. The word for it probably was desolation. Only an instant. She shook back her black hair and raised her chin, her mouth unmistakably the mocking mouth of Thady.

'Ah well,' she said, 'many chapters…'

They freewheeled down towards the city. The man from the North told Una he had decided against going on with the priesthood. He was just writing the last pages of his first book. There would be more, he assured her. He was indeed very sure. After that, Hannah and Una cycled together but spoke little. In Terenure, Hannah said, 'See you again, Una.' She and the softly decisive writer turned down a side road.

Nelson Forterre went on with Una as far as Harold's Cross. There they would take separate roads. He said, 'Let's stop just a minute.' They stood on the pavement by their bicycles. 'You should look into that business of the lectures, about getting time off from your department. Keep an open mind,' he said. 'I could look into the possibilities in Trinity, too, if you like.'

'Oh yes! Thanks. Do then…and I will ask about it.'

'We could compare notes—maybe by next Saturday we could have something to go on. I could ring you?'

'No phone at my digs.'

'Work?'

She gave him the number.

Another Saturday when she would not be joining in activities from the Craobh. She would meet them all an extra night during the week instead.

Beset with appetite. Is that what you'd call it?

Una Normile, Nelson Forterre.

In time, short time, these two persons had called it love. It was a word they used much between them. This, they had told each other, was what held them together, they, from their disparate backgrounds.

'Everything is relative,' Mrs Riverdale had insisted that day picking the blackcurrants. Una had had no idea what she meant. She saw the woman as a ginger-dyed lump of snobbery and affectation.

'What did she mean?' she asked Nelson some time later when she had got to know him better, 'with her absolute and relative, that Mrs Riverdale?'

'I absolutely love you,' he said by way of reply.

He had loved many women. He was twelve years older. What he said was comforting because of the disasters of her lank hair, the glasses she had to wear most of the time, her sallow skin. All her life she had longed to be beautiful in the style of the women in the bluish-tinted magazines from Chicago, or like Sadie O'Gorman, pink and cream and fair, whose father was the gombeen in Balnahown and who, before any of the other girls in the primary school knew anything about such things, seemed to know a great deal about matters between men and women.

'You are beautiful,' Nelson said. He was a truthful person, was he not? Therefore a miracle had been wrought. This was not her father, loving his childeen. This was a man who had come from a world far, in so many ways, from hers, who said he loved her and did not see her blemished as she had always considered herself to be. Beauty in the eye of the beholder. Healing to a lifelong wound.

But she remembers the city cousin telling her what he wanted her to do, Jack sniggering, a swollen purplish thing with revolting slime, an eternity of suffocation under the old clammy eiderdown, tightly held down. 'If you tell we will hold it down again,' they had said, 'and we won't let you out.' It had happened because she had longed to be included by Jack and the cousin. Inclusion had been at the price of this terrifying, shameful happening.

Contrary to earlier fantasies of enticing the male, she remains numb before desire. In her is no simple ready response.

'I wish it otherwise,' she tells Nelson. She wishes to rejoice in the natural flesh, with his riotous abandon.

'I've seen you rushing against the wind,' he said, 'a wild thing—that's how you are really.'

'The flesh is a hellish vileness—that is what I've been made to feel as long as I remember. I have told you about it all. With my head I know it false but still it's as if I have frozen up against this hellishness.'

'You will melt. I shall melt you.'

And he melted her.

Gladys Peach-Orr had asked them to her small glass-fronted place.

'It's what's called bijou—goes well with Gladys, don't you think?' Nelson said as they approached through the patio with its terracotta pots of plants.

Gladys's current lover Raymond was there, handsome, restless, long legs constrained at the small table. Gladys groomed—you could not but think of that beauty column expression—eyebrows perfect curves, nails flawlessly varnished, delicate ankles in sheer mesh above kid shoes. Wherefrom the coupons, let alone the price? And they would have to be black market rates. But of course she was a clever, self-sufficient earner with a well-to-do father to fall back on. A woman with everything. She was even kind. Would she be so without all the sufficiencies?

She presented steamed fish, a salad. No bread, no potatoes. After that, pears poached in wine.

'I loathe cooking, as you know, Nelson. I made a special effort for you. I mean both of you,' she gave a little bow to Una, smiling. Her teeth showed to advantage in the evening sun through the glass wall.

They were asked by other people to further entertainments: luncheons, teas, dinners, suppers. Nelson always ate with evident, if mannerly, zest.

'What do you do about returning hospitality?'

'People know my situation—as much as matters, that is to say they see me for the struggling—if belated—student which I am.'

'I feel awkward. I should bring things. What should I bring that might be suitable—that I can afford out of twenty-five shillings a week, rent paid?'

'From both of us, I bring Bewley's shortbread. Hadn't you noticed? It's wartime, butter and sugar rationed—people value Bewley's shortbread: good butter—Bewleys keep their own Jersey herd, you know.'

Late July 1942

'They've tackled me about Penn Reade. The Divinity School,' Nelson said a week later. 'He was right. And I somehow anticipated this. They don't like him. The Dean has spoken. Penn Reade, as I've told you, is *bête noire* in many places. has always met with much of that reaction. The very stuff he deals

195

with makes for mud-slinging.'

'How did they know about your interest in him?'

'Oh, I've been here a few years don't forget, and Trinity is a small world. Word gets around fast. Mrs Riverdale is one source. She abominates Penn Reade.

'I could see she might hate his plain speaking.'

'She and so many. It's a Swiftean city. The wits vie with one another. He's an obvious butt. As for Mrs Riverdale, she's wealthy. They like money in Trinity. The Dean often dines at her place.'

'I'm sure she abominates me too.'

He didn't deny it.

'The Dean asked if I had any, what he called, personal attachments. I spoke of you, said you were RC. This also went down badly. In fact, I got the feeling he already knew something, was just waiting for me to declare myself.'

'Unsuitable, surely?' the Dean had remarked, half-question, half-statement. He went on to wonder if Nelson had considered whether his…fiancée…would fit in with giving parish teas. The surface colouring was jocose but the heart of the matter was in dead earnest. The presiding over teas was vital.

'When you think of it,' Nelson said to Una, 'that's fair enough: teas are a community event and if one functions as a minister's wife, one is expected to participate in the giving of teas. I told you how much my mother did of that sort of thing. However, with the Dean I just laughed, leaving it in the air. Then he asked if you might be likely to turn Church of Ireland. Again I side-stepped—knowing the answer.'

'You were right. I wouldn't become Church of Ireland, I wouldn't suit parish teas at all. The Dean was also right.'

'So much for my tentative approaches to Divinity.'

There came a long silence.

'Well Nelson, what do you want? There's being a clergyman, on one side; on the other, Penn Reade—and me. What's your choice?'

'You're mocking me.'

'I'm not. I don't know enough to do that. I wish I did and could make all kinds of bright snappy comments.'

'Ah Una, thank heaven you don't. It's one of the reasons you're different. When you laugh I love it. I love your love of laughter. And I believe it; you weren't mocking. I'm tired of the hard glitter I meet so much of, flashing verbal darts, superficial stuff, often poisonous.'

Another silence.

'About the business of your being a clergyman, I'd have to say I hadn't really been very taken with it.'

'You never said.'

'I was trying to make it out, to work it out for myself. The one thing maybe I liked was the way it linked up with the Rydalls; I was always drawn to them, as you know. But their kind of existence would hardly be yours. And I cannot imagine myself, RC, ever fitting in.'

'Yes. I, too, have to say I have not been myself sure about it, about going all out for it. Ministry, yes, I take to the idea of ministering—doing things for people if I could, if I have it in me. And ministers—doubtless of varying merits—in my family going away back. But then again, more and more I feel formal religions of *any* brand are not for me. There are other ways to help.'

He stopped. There came again a long silence between them. Then he said. 'To utter a banality, I'm getting no younger. My mother finds me hopeless, trying this, that. But…exasperating as my pace may be, I am getting there, will get there in my own time. And time is relative—I remind myself of that as a comfort.'

Short pause.

'And you, Una, are you very impatient with me?'

What could she say? He was Nelson. He was of immense importance to her. That feeling seemed to encompass all the other mixtures of feelings inside her.

'I don't know that impatient is the right word.'

It was now late July.

Twenty

Una always wrote Mr and Mrs Normile on the envelope. About once every fortnight since coming to Dublin she wrote to them: Dear Mum and Dad. But Sean never wrote back. During her years in Marymount he had written her only three letters in all. She never doubted his affection because of this. She knew he disliked letter-writing as much as he did shopping: these things were Minnie's domain, as far as he was concerned. He wrote only those letters required by his post as teacher, by his position as owner of a hundred acres of mountainy land. When local people came to him for help in filling official forms and composing missives, he gave them every appearance of willingness. He took them to his closed room and never let them know that he found aiding in this way a nuisance.

The letter said: '...he is English and a Protestant...would it be all right for him to come to Balnahown for some of the time while I'm still there with you on my holidays?'

Minnie had shown it to Sean. The ridges set themselves up in his forehead as he read.

'God knows!' he said heavily. He put his head on his hand and stared away through the window to where the Shannon showed in the distance. 'Would you credit it?' he said after a while. 'I don't like it. She's asking for him to come for more than a week. Too sudden. Too soon. I don't like it. We like Protestants in their own place, but not this, not this.'

'Ah well, every generation brings its changes. She's young. Give the thing a chance. There's no harm in his coming. She'll be here for a week on her own first. We can maybe talk with her then.'

Words always came more readily to Minnie. Sean was nonplussed: how is a man to deal with such an unprecedented situation? Una herself had known that the very fact of her becoming a young woman had embarrassed him. Never a talker, he had no words easily available to speak to whatever female unapproachable reaches were entailed in her young womanhood. While she was still a child—ah childeen!—and in her very early teens, he and she had in common their great love of the land and all the features of nature manifested thereon. But the new dimension, the secret private development from child into woman kept Sean often tongue-tied with his daughter.

There was a scale of disgraces. Being on the dole was low on that scale. Minnie really pitied people on the dole. The district had many. God love them, Minnie said. Poverty—not due to booze, shiftlessness —was no disgrace. Nevertheless, to be on the dole was a disgracing thing, gnawed away self-respect. People on the dole expected to be looked down on.

Dirt was most definitely a disgrace. As to the locality of Balnahown, there was water to spare all over the region and soap was cheap: a small bit went a long way. The poorest children in her classes, brought up on the miserable dole, were sometimes the cleanest. She often remarked on this at home. She praised the efforts of the mothers. God reward them, she said. Those people with their hands stretched out to the dole-car at the corner of the school wall every Wednesday must need help with their self-respect, their plight must surely be humiliating. The thought of any of her own immediate kin having to be on the dole was petrifying: she would feel abased by such an actuality despite all her assertion that honest poverty was no disgrace.

Jail for criminal offences was certainly a disgrace to anyone. The stain of jail stuck to people if ever they got out. Could there be any hope of self-respect after the ignominy of such lowness.

A further disgrace so cancelled out any self-respect as to be spoken of only in the thinnest whispers or even to be indicated only by codes of grimaces, gestures and ambiguous terminology: the disgrace of pregnancy outside marriage.

'Watch out now, Maggie. Keep a guard on yourself. Remember your self-respect.' Minnie would admonish Maggie—inherently loose, she feared—who headed away on her evening out after the tasks were seen to.

Unmarried pregnant girls were unlikely to have had any self-respect in the first place. Their unspeakable plight had to be left to the mercy of heaven. It would be best if they could take their baggage and clear off out of the district altogether, for their staying on could lead only to scorn for them or acid patronising in the years to come.

The worst of all was apostasy. Within the parish of Moygrane, with its outlying western stretch of Balnahown, there had never been an apostate. 'Heaven be praised for that,' Minnie and her abiding friends would say. Nor had ever a case been cited in returned emigrants. Even the 'Baron' McCoy who, after forty years, brought home briefly a huge automobile from the United States full of women in filmy dresses and picture hats, even he kept the faith.

Whenever he stopped the car to show them the boggy scenery, the ladies emerged on the roadsde to the immense delight of any who witnessed, they being showpieces of a rarer order. He had got the vehicle blessed by the priest. When he and his bevy had gone away again to make more money in Chicago, the photo of the blessing—it showed the 'Baron', his gauzy ladies of joy, the priest, and the automobile receiving the dappling of holy water— still hung in O'Gorman's pub.

'You haven't written about the *Craobh* in a long time,' Minnie said.

'I suppose I haven't, Mam.'

'How is that now?'

'Ah it's that I haven't been going there as much. They were—some of them—getting political.'

'Isn't that a pity? Losing touch with the girls from Marymount too. *They* wouldn't be going political surely? Nice girls they were, your previous school companions.'

An oblique castigation of her taking up with Nelson. Minnie, up to this time, always said that she had forgiven England of the present for the hideous injustices of the past. England of the present signified a source of employment for many leaving Ireland who otherwise would have nothing at home but the few shillings on the dole, one of the lowest disgraces. Since the wireless had come into the house, England had further meant the BBC which Minnie so much enjoyed: the special accent, classical music and other music—Mastrovani in Palm Grove, Henry Hall and all. This new Englishman of the present, she had no idea what he'd be like. She was ready to give him benefit of the doubt. The whole supremely important matter of religion, though…

Her contact with Protestants had been the Rydalls, the Deerings, the couple of decent, modestly farming families in the neighbourhood—Drescoes, Longshoots. She had no fault to find with any of them. They kept to themselves, spinsters and bachelors, a dwindling breed. Amongst them, there had been no attempt ever at courting, or inter-marrying with Catholics. There was nothing wrong with being civil to Protestants. Look at those Palatine farmers to the east of Moygrane; they got on with everyone. Straight, honest people, willing to lend a neighbourly working hand if they could. Look at the way the Rydalls and the Normiles always were good friends. The Protestants in the city, too, you never heard bad of them; they minded their own business and were pleasant to the Catholics around them. So long as religion was kept in its place, things could be managed very well. Once you crossed the bounds you were in a quagmire. Very soon you could be sucked into hell.

The one Protestant who had married a local girl, Sadie O'Gorman's cousin, was not from the district. The girl had met him in England, where he was retired from the British army because of injuries: he had just three fingers to his right hand and always needed a walking stick. Before their marriage he had had the grace to turn Catholic without the slightest objection. A credit to Sadie O'Gorman's cousin. Wasn't it a great victory for the faith?

Minnie wouldn't say anything yet to Una about that side of things.

It had continued to be a good summer. This was Una's first evening home after six months. No one mentioned Nelson during the evening meal. You could tell from faces that he was very much there in everyone's mind. Including Maggie's: she was bound to have listened in; she was like that. Jack had not appeared. Una had not seen him since the day in May when she had told him about meeting Hannah in Stephen's Green, her changed plans, about the proposed gathering in the Pine Forest which the man from the North had organised. Through Hannah, Jack, indeed, had been inadvertently the cause of her meeting Nelson.

'Where's Jack?'

'Oh don't you know Jack,' Minnie said. 'Always down the glen in that old dugout of his when he's not out fishing or up to something in his room. He comes when the hunger drives him.'

Una offered help with the washing-up but Maggie said, 'Ah, go off and enjoy yourself. Isn't it your holiday?'

It was hard to feel close to Maggie. In fact, you didn't think you'd ever manage that. Since the incidents of the matches and the cracked clock, you never trusted her. You wondered about her, about the ways people were separated from one another. You felt even less inclined now than before to trust Maggie. Maggie would have done very well for herself if she had had the chance of extra schooling. She was cute as a fox. Would have made as clever a lawyer as Gladys Peach-Orr. Better. But she was not someone you would like to talk to about Nelson, the problems that seemed to be made by his different nationality and backgrond, including religion. The whole district would have a hundred versions of him within hours.

Una said, 'Thanks Maggie. OK. I'll go and find

Jack.'

She took off in the direction of the dugout. Soon she saw Jack coming towards the house.

'You're getting hungry then,' she said, by way of greeting.

'What are *you* up to?' He looked angry.

'I'm coming to see you, what else?'

'That's not what I mean and you know it. What's this about you and some Protestant English bloke?'

'Well I suppose it's what you say—he *is* Protestant and he *is* English.'

'What do you want doing a thing like that for? Last time I saw you, you were head and heels into that Irish club, spouting Irish morning, noon and night.'

'And you, the supposedly Irish man, made a mock of all that. Things happen. You were all for nihilism and such isms then. And that doesn't tie in with the way you are going on now, this way you are reacting.'

He looked even angrier. 'Always Miss Smart.' He had not been angry like this with her for a very long time. It was as if they were back in the days when he used to savage her for being born at all.

'Ah Jack, come on. I never thought you'd be like this about it.'

'*And* taking up with psychoanalysis. Crackpot stuff. You'll have to be told fair and square that no doctor in this country would go along with that phoney stuff. A load of quackery.'

'I know. I already know about the attitude of the doctors. And of the bishops. And, it seems, most other people.'

'Leaving your religion. Turning your back on everyone.'

'What do you mean, leaving my religion? We have always been friendly with the Protestants—the Rydalls, the Deerings...'

She was not going to be angry back. She was not angry. She was dismayed.

'That,' Jack said, 'is a different thing altogether.'

'I could say you're the one turning your back on people, finding fault—shopkeepers, doctors, clergy, professors, sticking a knife into this one, that one. You have been the born faulter, always criticising, turning your back on everyone except *your* chosen few.'

She was shaken to find how vulnerable she still was before his ferocity in this new phase. To be outraged for the sake of their traditional religion was quite unlike him. Never had he shown the slightest support of anything to do with it beyond a token, a grudging compliance with attending Mass on Sundays. It was unlikely he still went to confession or communion any more, now that he had been so long away from the surveillance of Sean and Minnie.

It was that time of a fine summer evening when all the essences of the bogland wafted on the gently cooling air. The sun was going down to the suffused horizon, west of the pinkish strip of Shannon. A lark let free its last fling of the day. Across the *reidh*, a *gowreen roe* called several times in its low flight. Over the boundary ditch by what used to be the Whelan's land, now the property of Tony's uncle, a corncrake signalled intermittently. From where she and Jack were standing in the rushes, Sean could be seen going up the boreen to the iron gate that led out to the bye road. He would have finished his pipe by now, having walked back and forth on the level patch outside the house. He would soon stand at the high point near the gate, and look out over the land until the dark closed in.

She was at home again in Balnahown: the place of enormous meaning, the people who had always been nearest. Balnahown and they, together, were a force made up of loves, rancours, things not to be understood, the power of which would always work upon her. An enduring force.

'And all this blather about his ancestry. You know what I think about that?'

'I do. And he thinks the same. More or less. Can anyone choose in the matter of birth. You could talk to him, couldn't you, instead of flying off the handle before you ever met him?

They were moving towards the house through the rushes, past the spring-water well. She tried to change the subject.

'The exam results weren't so bad, after all. You'll have to repeat only one thing. I'm glad about that, Jack. You'll be finished soon.'

He said nothing, not to be mollified by her congratulatory tone.

'Great for Mam and Dad too.'

He still said nothing. They both knew that he had taken far longer than necessary in getting this far, that he had caused Minnie and Sean a great deal of worry. Her congratulating could be taken as an implicit reminder of where she had scored over him, old tricks in subtler form.

'Will this Nelson fellow—what a name! Cripes!— well, will he be great for them too?'

This time it was she who made no reply. Would Nelson be great for Minnie and Sean?

According to what Nelson himself said he'd plagued his mother in plenty getting where he was. She was to be plagued again with the news of Una Normile.

And where were they going, Nelson Forterre and Una Normile?

Twenty-one

He had brought his bicycle on the train and cycled up the hill from Moygrane. He was wearing his oldest baggy flannels and tweed jacket with scuffed leather patches on the worn out elbows. The clothes he was easiest in. Both garments, once of good stuff, were cast-offs from 'connections'. Under his bed in Trinity were battered leather suitcases, stamped with Forterre. They contained odds and ends of garments passed on by relatives. 'One must not waste,' he said to Una, 'particularly in wartime. They'll turn in usefully yet.' He continued to draw on them.

From the saddlebag, after an appropriate interval, he produced for Minnie two rectangles of Bewley's shortbread wrapped in waxed paper, a few packets of Petersen's pipe cleaners for Sean, fishing flies for Jack, who was not present.

'Ah now why did you do that?' Minnie said, her customary utterance when acknowledging a gift.

Habitually awkward on receiving a favour, Sean said, 'Thanks, thanks, thanks,' his usual response at such a time.

Nelson said, 'It's very good of you to let me come.' To this, neither Minnie nor Sean made a reply, none coming readily. His being there was outside a day-to-day situation to be met with pat phrases. For them, for him.

It seemed plain he was shy. It seemed, too, he had manners: Minnie highly valued manners. He carried trays for her, buckets for Maggie. It further seemed he took an interest in everything: the school, the methods of teaching, in the way the household ran, the yard, the farm, Peetie. He weeded drills for Sean in the small kitchen garden: they could be heard talking together through the open door of the kitchen. He helped Peetie tackle the horses.

In due time he gave Jack the fishing flies.

'I don't fish myself now but I used to—changed about it.'

Jack was unforthcoming, did not inquire why he no longer fished. Nelson brought up the subject of boats.

'I see Una has been priming you on likely topics.' Jack's tone was more or less saying you'll find no country goms around here.

'Well, isn't it what people do, talk about their families? Isn't it natural that you came into the talk? Besides, I do a bit of freelancing—all is grist. Always on the lookout for an article.'

Jack looked him over. Maybe the old clothes helped. Jack did not, as well he might have done, give an inference that the bloody English toff was dressing down to bogtrotter level. Bloody patronising. Instead he said, 'Since you've no fear of it then, come on down through the mud and see…what's to see.'

'Good common sense,' Minnie retorted when Maggie slyly said, 'I see Nelson doesn't bother about style.'

Maggie was longing for a good long gossip about this different creature. She would get only short answers, she knew, to any questions.

'But what,' Minnie said to Sean when no one was about, 'is to happen when it comes to Sunday? Will he go to Mass, do you think? And if he does, has he nothing better to show the neighbours?' These questions she had not put to Una.

'Ah-sha, 'tisn't the clothes that matter,' Sean replied. 'Will he go at all, that's the thing.'

He was right, of course, Minnie had to concede, to herself. As to appearances when going to Mass, the schoolchildren were always taught that to be clean was enough if that was the best people could manage. But to have patches going out of the Normile house to Mass was unheard of. All her life Minnie had made strenuous efforts to ensure her family were a credit going to the church on Sunday.

On Saturday evening when Nelson was down the glen with Jack—for Jack had capitulated to the degree of asking him to come and help with something in the dugout—Una set out the ironing blanket on the table to press thereon, under a damp cloth, a second, better-looking pair of trousers which Nelson had brought. And although Minnie had made no mention of her worries, Una held up the finished work for her to see.

'There you are now, Mam, he won't disgrace you tomorrow at Mass. There's a good jacket too, on a hanger since he came—no wrinkles.'

'Well now…' was all Minnie said. To find her anxieties regarding the matter of Nelson's intentions for Sunday and his turnout for the day allayed all at once seemed to put her at a loss. Tentatively, as though it were too much of an intimacy, she brushed a finger against the folded trouser-leg. 'Good material in those,' she remarked, trying to give an impression of nonchalance, as though she had never had a bothering thought.

Minnie was shelling peas.

'Wild as an unfettered animal, that used to be the way with her,' she was saying, 'climbing trees, never a shoe, full of cuts and bruises from tearing through bushes and brambles.'

Having put iodine on the gashes, Una came on them to find Nelson smiling, sitting on the grass by the two strange stones, helping with the shelling. Minnie was sitting on a kitchen chair. It was good to see them thus happily arranged, to hear her mother reminiscing affectionately about her for his benefit. She was barefoot today also. At Balnahown in summer she was mostly barefoot. Earlier that day, taking him further afield, she had rushed to jump a fence and tripped, getting two jagged cuts on her legs from barbed wire. The outcome was Minnie's reminiscing.

Later, after the evening meal, and as twilight closed in, Nelson Forterre and Una Normile rambled away towards the moorland, west.

'Wild as an unfettered animal? Mmm. We'll see about that. See if you can escape now.'

'I want to marry her, Mr Normile.'

Minnie was there too. Sean did not lift his head. He was waiting for Minnie to make the first move. This was excruciating territory.

'You know, Nelson, that there are certain requirements, that our church is very strict on these matters,' Minnie said.

'I do know. I am thinking most seriously about that. Keeping an open mind.'

He left a week before she did. They had tramped the bogland and glens. They had cycled down Kiridyne, they had pushed the bicycles up Cloonard. Word had it in the surrounding countryside that Una Normile was to be seen tearing up hill and down dale with some fella with a posh accent and not a stitch to his back, going around the bogs in rags and patches—and this in spite of Nelson's respectable jacket and pressed trousers at the Sunday Mass: a beggarly figure suited better the local spice. She was engaged, it was said, but, for sure, he wasn't any leg-up for the Normiles, this bloke. What would the pair of them live on, Mother of God! She'd have to let the civil service job go by the board, for that was the way of things, the way the country was run. And what class of money could he be earning and the cut of him?

They had gone to fetch the batteries for the wireless from Mr Rydall.

It was clear Nelson and the Rydalls were easy with one another. The ease had much to do with their similarities as to breeding, accent, the old comfortable clohes, places travelled. Elfrida asked them to tea. The parrot was still on his perch.

'They can live to be a hundred and more, you know,' Elfrida said. Her orange hair was allowed now to be grey. Instead of the cloche hat she wore a silk turban on this occasion while dispensing tea.

'Protestants are nicer,' Una had said to Minnie after Andrew had clapped hands having, without her knowing, watched her shin up a tree by the rectory and slither down again. 'Well done, old girl!' He had held the door of the Ford open for her as he would do for a lady, when she was only a child. He had carefully attended her at tea, putting a little table beside her chair. It was so very, very sad about Andrew. Awful. There had been little of him left after the air raid, Minnie had told her. Elfrida and her brother—especially Mr Rydall—looked thinner and older. In between bouts of anecdote, Mr Rydall had an absent look, needing a question to bring him back.

With Una to themselves again, Minnie and Sean enjoined her to pray for the conversion. Sean did this once only, and only with Minnie present as a ballast. Telling anyone to pray was unnerving. Giving out the Rosary was not the same thing; it was not a personal, face-to-face matter. It was a ritual in which the strain of daily confrontation was absorbed. You could announce prayers for this and that intention during the rosary and no one need feel embarrassed: faces were hidden in hands or by the back of the one in front of you. In exhorting Una, Minnie did not suffer discomfiture as did Sean. She urged Una daily to pray for grace for Nelson to do the right thing.

'You know we cannot agree to the marriage unless he turns.'

'But if he agrees that the children are RC?'

'We want a conversion. There has to be a conversion.'

'God knows that's it.' On this last time before she was to return to Dublin, Sean quickly supported Minnie.

'Well he has promised to look into all of it.'

'Looking into is not enough.'

'Tis true, 'tis true,' said Sean. They were adamant.

Curiously, they had not once yet brought up the issue of income. That of religion had been paramount. Almost as if it were an afterthought Minnie now queried, 'And what were the two of you going to live on? You know well that a woman in the civil service has to give up her job if she marries.'

'I know.'

'Well, what then?'

What indeed? About her taking up a course in Trinity College she had not dared say a word either to them or Jack. A hurricane would strike. Church ruling forbade Catholics to study at Trinity—without specific permission it meant excommunication. The reality—that a few were always to be found studying there—would not mitigate her proposed transgression in the eyes of her parents, of her brother. Jack, the vaunted existentialist, the puzzling reactionary.

'We wouldn't be marrying just yet,' she rejoined. How could they? Her wages were utterly vital to the fees. And Nelson had insisted that he would help somehow to make up the sum.

'Nelson is hoping for better pay.'

Yes, he was hoping. But on what foundation?

He had said, 'I'll find it, you'll see. Have faith.'

Faith. She was beginning to look into the concept of faith. One of the cardinal virtues, so it had always been drummed into your ears. The many sermons on it had not really helped her to feel it so.

Minnie had always been the letter-writer. Nevertheless, her letters were never as relaxed as her conversation. When she wrote she seemed more self-consciously the schoolteacher, mindful of correct expression, too often to the detriment of her innate liveliness; the letters lacked the vividness and ripple of her daily speech. Nelson was serious matter. More than ever were Minnie's letters constrained since his imperative conversion severely pressed inside her head. Sean was bleakly stiff in the scant missives he forced himself to pen to his son and daughter. The subject of Nelson was so sensitive that he could not bring himself to write anything at all of it to Una.

September 1942

He had gone to the Jesuits. He was most concientious. He sifted meticulously the requirements. He was thorough.

Una wrote telling Minnie. She got back prayerful letters: it was a blessed thing he was doing. Una must continue her storming of heaven as they did. They were offering Mass, Rosaries, visits to the Blessed Sacrament. Minnie had undertaken novenas.

'That priest is a really fine man. I like him immensely. He is cultured. Far too clever, too subtle to attempt anything like prosletyising. But I cannot do it, Una. I've gone into it all. I'll write, myself, to your parents. I'll tell them.'

He did.

The reaction was as Una had feared.

'They will not change,' she said.

'No, I don't think they will.'

'I hate to hurt them.'

'I know. I don't want to. I hate to. But…that's how it is.'

'Well…'

'Not well…I know it's not well.'

'Maybe we shouldn't have said anything to them—about marrying. Giving them more worries at this stage…I'm thinking about the way money is between us. With our joint money the way it is didn't we know we wouldn't be marrying yet anyhow? There are the fees for Trinity. We should have stayed quiet about marrying. A four-year course I've taken on. I'll be twenty-three before I'm through with Trinity. Will we still want to marry?'

'I will.'

'How do you know?'

'I will. I won't change about you. Yes, I know you're thinking I've changed about many things along the line but you are in a different category. About you I won't change. But money could change...there will be more money...'

'We hope. We're hoping for money. Could there be any hope of understanding all round? Hope is also a cardinal virtue.'

Faith. Hope. Charity. Up to now they had been an easy cant, rattled off in catechism class. The word 'cardinal', used in this way, explained. It had not really meant anything. Ages after, you think about these things learnt by rote. Charity—what did they all, herself, Nelson, Mam, Sean, Jack, know about charity? Love thy neighbour as thyself. They wouldn't want her to be even friendly with Nelson now: Charity was subject to condition. The pale, impassioned youg man at the *Craobh* shouting 'Blood must flow again!' Mrs de Burca wanting a companion through the dreadful night. Love thy neighbour. The cardinal virtues. Formulae readily spun off in class. So complicated—impossible?—to try to apply.

Nelson said, 'Whatever about understanding— and money—there will be no trouble legally in getting married then.'

'If we are still of a marrying mind.'

Breath. How foul so much of it is. How unsettling to think one might walk about, unconscious of one's own noxious airs—like the recruiting nun at Marymount, the boss on a Monday morning with his sour beer and onion exhalations. You dread to think you risk being such a source of miasma.

But behind the breath the boss was decent. Heart of gold. From the first when by appointment she told him, ensconced in his private compartment, about her access to Trinity, her great wish to avail of that with the blessing of brasshats, he had pulled the necessary strings. He had nothing to say about church rulings. He himself was Protestant, the civil service mercifully being non-denominational. As a result of his machinations, the Department was permitting her space for the required minimal attendance at lectures.

'Don't shout about it. Best kept low,' the boss said.

But word always filters. Kitty—Una's office saviour in the line of totting—blew prettily on her drying nail varnish, obliquely eyed Una's long column, wrongly totted as usual, and said, 'A genius 'tis we have amongst us. Trinity College will be blessed.'

Twenty-two

October 1942

Jack had returned to Mrs Breen's. He was resitting the part failed in his finals.

Although sleeping under the same roof, Una and he rarely met, each involved so much in individual preoccupations. She had been to the *Craobh* only twice since her holiday in Balnahown. The activities there which had previously absorbed her seemed irrelevant to the way her life had been going recently. It was a way she did not want to discuss with anyone there, not with the old friends from Marymount, nor the new friends. An added reason for her absence was that on her last visit they had told her they themselves were seriously thinking of leaving; they did not like the political colouring increasingly there, governing what had been for them and Una a source of fun and enjoyment of the language. She seemed to have taken into herself Sean's aversion to politics and wanted no part of them. Neither, for their own reasons, did the friends.

It was the day for her first lecture in Trinity. Her lunch period had been stretched a little to fit it in. Before the lecture, she was to swallow her rapid sandwich in Nelson's rooms.

'If I'm not there—and I may not be and wife will have the door locked—you could eat it in College Park. We'll meet later anyway, as we said, for your first impressions.'

As she rushed down steps from the civil service

building she was amazed to see Jack waiting at the bottom for her. Never once before had he come to find her there. Staff members were all about, coming and going on their lunch break. It was the custom with many to buy small gooey cakes in Johnston, Mooney & O'Brien and go off to eat them in Stephen's Green. Merrion Square, although to hand, was a closed elitist patch of green, accessible only to privileged members.

Of all days, it was not one on which she was glad to find Jack standing there.

'Jack! I'm in a terrible rush...' Of course she had told him nothing about her undertaking in Trinity.

'We'll go down a bit here, get away from this mob of pen-pushers.' He moved off towards Merrion Square. The direction was right but why, of all days, did he slow her up like this?

'You know we can't go in there...' He was looking for a way to open one of the gates into the exclusive greenery. 'Come on, Jack, we'll talk as we walk...I've things to do.'

'They tell me from home he's not turning.'

'He isn't.'

'And you're still carrying on with him.'

'Carrying on is not what I'd call it.'

'You're not to. You're under age.'

'So what of it? It's no business of yours, Jack.'

'I'm making it my business. They asked me to.'

'Well, keep trying.'

She suddenly sped down the street, not stopping until she got to Nelson's rooms. He might or might not be there. He was. And no wife in the way. Eating porridge. His cheap but nourishing lunch.

'It's best I move out of Mrs Breen's.' She was panting and sweating. 'We'll have to look for a room.'

Jack had not followed. Promising intervention to Sean and Minnie did not include galloping through Lincoln Gate and the grounds of Trinity College in pursuit of a female, to the hawing and cawing of the snooty bloody fecks in there.

The split in *Craobh an Dóchais* had materialised. Branch of Hope: what did it stand for now? The friends had left to join another body of *Conradh na Gaeilge*. A new name was given to the eruptive who remained in the old premises.

'Won't you join with us, Una?' The friends wanted her.

'We don't see much of you these days, Una.'

She felt guilty.

I do love the Irish language. I am indeed fond of my friends.

Or is it that I needed them? Friends are a way of protecting yourself. Was it that their company was necessary for me, new in the city? Not to have it said I had no one? Was not popular? To be seen to be liked, is that more important to me than for me, in actuality, to like people? I had serious thoughts of leading an ascetic life in an enclosed order. And when I worked through that, I still imagined myself a reasonably middle-of-the-road Catholic. Catholicism decrees I must not marry Nelson Forterre or it makes it very difficult for me to do so. It claims the children. Do I still believe in the preached infallibility of one man? Is his speaking *ex cathedra* something I must be governed by? All my religious teaching says I must. I begin to question. I love discovering; I am curious. Much that I discover divides me, sets up battles in me. Conflicts.

She was nearer understanding what had been a threatening question from Mrs Riverdale, frightening because she felt ignorant in face of it. In Balnahown, in Marymount, with Jack, Thady Keane, 'ignorant' was a term of utter contempt. An ignorant *bostoon*, an ignorant hussy—low despicable creatures. In the face of Mrs Riverdale's question, she had not wanted to be shown stripped, ignorant; she had had no answering experience nor mental training to give, or fabricate, some abstract cleverness. 'Do you believe in absolute or relative?' She felt nearer now to realising there were grounds for such a query. At the time she had further disliked Mrs Riverdale because of it, had felt it as another of her pretensions. Now, she still saw it as difficult to answer but for different reasons—changes coming fast about her, altering experiences.

But she would never reveal anything of this to Mrs Riverdale. That woman, her bald son, her exquisite daughter, would laugh derisively at tentative approaches. Mrs Riverdale was a bitch. Was she an absolute bitch? 'Why is Nelson Forterre throwing himself away on an ignorant peasant girl?' Yes, in roundabout ways it had been told back to her; the inference was 'when a delectable, wealthy, Oxford-educated Riverdale daughter is available'. That woman did seem an absolute bitch, yes.

Yet the dyed hair, heavily powdered blotchy face, loud manner, were they not signs of vulnerability? The brittle flippancy, the flirtatious foibles pathetically meant to titillate young men, what went on beneath them? Was the weighty gift of fruit at parting ostentation or generosity? Was she only relatively a bitch?

Mr Riverdale seemed what you could call a decent

man. Absolutely decent? What had made him so wealthy? Gladys Peach-Orr was a charmer. For some: for their loverly period only? As soon as that was past, would she be for them a bitch?

There might seem to be no absolutes.

She paid Mrs Breen, who looked both worried and curious, and then she left, not having seen Jack. The room she was going to was a big improvement on her sharing the cluttered space of Mrs Breen's bedroom. It was a place temporarily vacated by one of Nelson's friends. You got to it via a black outside wooden staircase. The space beneath, a padlocked store of some kind, seemed to be packed with a miscellany of bits and pieces, obscured by layers of cobwebs on the single window. Only a few other of the small mews buildings in the row seemed to be vaguely occupied.

That night she posted a note to Minnie giving her new address. 'More space for me here, Mam. I was very squashed in Mrs Breen's.' This was true, if not the reason for moving. But then she didn't say it was, did she? She did not refer to Jack's accosting her on their behalf. Nor to Nelson. For the following two days she went to work as usual, keeping a sharp look-out for Jack, fitting in one afternoon lecture in Trinity. Nelson came in the evening but did not stay.

'It is better I don't until we see how things develop.'

On the evening of the third day, there was a knock on the door to the laneway: Nelson must have forgotten his key. Outside in the lane stood Jack, Minnie and Sean.

'So this is your set-up,' Jack said.

'We are taking you home,' Minnie said.

'We are that,' Sean said.

223

'We are telling the Department you are sick.'

'You can say that again,' Jack said.

'We are keeping you at home till you come to your senses.'

'I might have known, the way his eyebrows nearly met. Behind eyebrows like that there's always a plotting nature.' While he was still in Balnahown, Minnie had commended Nelson's eyebrows for their clear line.

'Put your things together and come on now. No trying to dodge; it won't work.'

Their words followed on one another without a break. She said nothing. She placed a note on the table. 'I've had to go.'

'Let me see what you are writing there.'

She was back in Marymount, having her letters inspected by Mother Immaculata.

She was, of course, a minor, legally.

Jack and Sean stood guard while she got into the Ford. They arranged between them: Jack would go on her bicycle back to Mrs Breen's. In the morning, Sean and Minnie—Mrs Breen was somehow making space for them overnight—would take her and her belongings to Balnahown in the car.

'You are officially on sick leave,' Minnie said. 'You'll have time to come to your senses down in Balnahown.'

If she pumped every so often maybe the bike would just get her there in spite of the slow puncture. She wouldn't phone Nelson until she got to Dublin. But money she had as good as none. In the fretwork casket to hold odds and ends which Sean once made for Minnie, she found a few shillings. Taking them was something she hated doing. She stemmed guilt by resolving to pay back later in a postal order.

Peetie and the extra man were far out of sight putting finishing touches to the potato pits. She waited until Maggie was safely on her way to them with tea. There was a hunk of brown bread on the kitchen table. She shoved it into her pocket. Avoiding the usual road to Moygrane, taking the roundabout way, she set off. But once out of Moygrane, she would have to take the main road: it was quickest and the puncture might be liable to worsen on devious routes.

Should they come upon her, she did not know what she would do. She kept envisaging Sean overtaking her in the car. She was comparatively safe if they thought she had taken the bike with her on the train: they would wire Jack to be at Kingsbridge station. When Jack reported back her non-appearance, further measures would be taken, but before that she would have had some start. She would not think about the hundred and sixty miles.

It was a rapid spin down Kiridyne Hill. On such a sharp cloudless evening, promising frost later, a spin like it should have been exhilarating. Not this day. She was too troubled and confused. Also, she was physically very uncomfortable, much too hot, having put on layers of clothes, the best way to carry them since the bicycle was her only conveyance. Once she had decided, she did not wait to search out any kind of carrier bag and straps to fasten it firmly to the bicycle. Speed mattered. A bottle of water she had not remembered; she became very thirsty but would not stop anywhere yet to ask for a drink.

Without lamp or torch she should not really travel after dark. As she got past Nenagh, it began to darken rapidly. She went down a side road and found a ditch where it might be possible to stay till dawn. It was freezing hard now. She had brought the bike down into the hollow with her. But sleep was not possible on the frozen lumpy ground, cold penetrating to the marrow despite the layers of garments. Far too much on parts and nothing on her numb legs but a pair of ankle socks. She would have to search further. Hay was warm. Ahead was a farmhouse, a barn.

Hay rustles, crackles. While she was doing her utmost to make a noiseless ascent, a dog heard or smelled. He barked—many times. She would be discovered. The bike was down there. There was most likely an SOS on the wireless. A man could be heard coming from the house, walking around the yard and calling the dog. A woman had now come out to join him.

'A fox, I suppose.'

'I'd say. But them hens is as safe as ever. No fox can get 'em. No fear. There's not even a geek outa them. Listen.'

The dog had stopped. The hens made no clamour. There was only the silence of the starry frosty night. The man and woman returned to the house. The door was closed.

In the hay it was warmer but real sleep was impossible. Her clothes seemed to have become alive to attack with a million sharp prickles of hard stalks. At the first faint touch of dawn, she crept down from the barn and stole away. The tyre was flat but stayed firm after pumping. If it went totally flat…that was unthinkable.

A description of her would be on the wireless—in spite of what that might mean to her parents in the humiliation of district gossip, their concern for her eternal soul would mean more. Her salvation was at stake. She was causing them bitter trouble. She was breaking their hearts. She was about to wound them further. She had never wanted to. If only they would leave her to work out things with Nelson...

People in garages and shops kept their wirelesses going. She must look very odd: people would notice her queer bulky padded shape, her nervousness, her blue legs. How much would it cost to get a puncture mended? For the first time she was struck with the fact that she had never had to pay for this: at Balnahown, Peetie or Jack or Sean always mended punctures and, since her being in Dublin, the need had not even once arisen in spite of all the cycling— and that was probably why the tyre was almost worn out now. She did not want to stop and ask anywhere for anything and wanted to keep the few shillings for trying to phone Nelson in Dublin. Her aim was to get within local phoning distance before the printing works closed at five. Things might not work that way, the money might be needed.

She pedalled rapidly. In the dawn of an autumn day the road was quiet. During the night she had chewed the hunk of bread, more to fill in some of the dragging hay-needled hours than from hunger. As the day advanced the sun was bright; the sun of frosty days. Too bright. Her eyes grew tired. The saddle hurt, her legs ached; once again the weight of garments had her sweating. The hay which had worked its way in, pricked at every move. She paused only to pump the tyre, to relieve herself. But somewhere between Portlaoise and Kildare, thirst and weariness finally brought her to stop at a one-storey wayside house. A woman with a couple of children behind her came to the door.

'Would you please give me a drink and a slice of bread? I am very sorry to trouble you.' She was being like a tinker. She would see tinkers with new sympathy from this on.

The woman looked puzzled. This was not the kind of beggar she was used to. Una knew she was taking a risk by asking. A wireless could be heard from inside. The woman said, 'Come in.' She pointed to a chair at the table. She asked no question but put a cup of milk and two slices of buttered brown bread on a plate in front of Una. The children aged about three and four just looked on, making no sound. A strange visitation.

'I am really grateful to you. I wish I could pay you.'

Again the woman appeared puzzled but did not look directly at Una.

'Goodbye.' But there was no reply.

Una kept searching the horizon to her right for the first view of the Dublin hills. At last, just as the tyre needed pumping yet again—she had lost count of the times—there they showed. The sight of them gave some renewal of energy.

She phoned from the first telephone box in Inchicore.

'Nelson.'

'Good God! Where are you? But…say no more. People are on the watch. Can you be at the usual place in a half-hour?'

'I think so.'

'All right.'

He rang off. It was like a thriller. Cryptic. Like spies. But she was too exhausted and troubled to feel any stimulus in that aspect of the situation, to feel anything but the wish to see him and sink down somewhere to rest. He would take on the future.

The usual place. That meant his rooms in Trinity.

She did not have to reach them, quite, for he was there, waiting, in the entrance archway. He was a little back from the opening, staring out, his face tense under the old shooting cap. It had turned to rain: his oilskin cape and her gabardine coat probably helped to make them unremarkable, to blend with the other rainproofed people hurrying past. But he spoke urgently:

'Una, I'm sorry, but we must keep moving. People have been to me several times today—Jack, the police, a priest. When you weren't on the train last night—Jack met it—a search was set in motion. No wonder, of course. But the point is they could be back. And again, naturally. So since you phoned I've been in touch with the Reades—we'll go there.'

Another six miles to cycle. Too tired to think, she followed behind his bicycle until they got clear of the heaviest traffic. He called over his shoulder to her then, 'It's very difficult to talk now. But just believe me, it's best to go to the Reade's place.'

She was beyond questioning. The long ride, the punctured tyre, lack of sleep, turmoil in the head, hunger—all combined to make her a dull lump swathed in three sweaters and two skirts under her gaberdine coat, creaking automatically on and on. She did not want to go to the Reades' but her going there had to be accepted, like so many other things, in the belief that Nelson was acting for the best, that she herself was, in her attachment to him. Amongst other things, to be for the present accepted, was sorrow at hurting Sean and Minnie. She loved them. Greatly. She was hurting them: being with Nelson, the non-Catholic, in defiance af all the dicta of her religion, meant this.

Penn Reade had said to Nelson, 'The first thing to do is send a telegram to say she is safe. One can well imagine their anxiety. They must be racked with worry. Send it as soon ever as you can. Then, she is under-age: the next thing tomorrow is to go to a solicitor—I know a good one. You could be charged with abduction or we could, since she is here in the house. Things must be managed within the law. I'll go with you both. And I think it advisable she does not go out alone. The hierarchy is powerful. Actual abduction of another dimension could happen and be seen as perfectly correct, or blessed delivery from evil.'

Twenty-three

In the Phoenix Park were long double lines of stacked turf bordering the green acres. They stretched past *Áras an Uachtaráin*, the President's stately residence. The stacked turf brought from the bogs of the Republic was a government expedient as a reserve. At any time, crisis was possible in the neutral country of Ireland, depending on unforeseeable turns of the war. The Americans were, after all, in the North. Coal was severely rationed; at any time, sources of supply from England could be cut off completely. Men were employed to patrol the stacks as a safeguard against theft. One of the people who gathered together every Friday night at Penn Reade's house earned his living at present as one of the patrol band.

Dublin was a cold city in November 1942. The room Penn Reade worked in doubled as a family place when he had finished in the evening. Apart from it, the whole house was cold.

When she read in her cubicle—the only sleeping space available—Una used a hot water bottle, wrapped in position at the back of her legs by the gabardine coat turned into a kind of rug, firmly folded around her from the waist down.

In Cornwall, Mrs Forterre, shrunken beside her feeble fire of damp logs and thinking of the distances, at all levels, between her and him who once was her so darling sonny, thinking of lost fortunes and her present isolation, took what comfort she could from

231

the decades old fur coat tucked about her stiffened knees.

Even getting the water heated for the rubber bottle Una found to be difficult. With gas rationed, there was only the 'glimmer' in the off-hours. Illegal to use. Inspectors went round. But people sneaked it all the same. Una Normile became a sneak in the Reade house. Sometimes. Depending on the ravages of cold. Also there, to avail of, was the scarcely alive layer of slack, low in the dining room grate. You could warm a few cups of water on it. Kettles and saucepans became irretrievably blackened. Beatrice attempted an interminable simmer in the grate a few times. This did not work, the pressure of the pot crushing out what feeble life struggled in the slack. Beatrice was a dutiful ineffectual cook at the best of times. She made no claims otherwise.

All sorts came to the Friday nights. One of them, an enterprising citizen, envisaging a market for it in the times that were, thought up a new kind of hay-box. He employed a number of people on his enterprise. A nicely turned out middle-aged woman, acting for him, arrived by arrangement to demonstrate on one of the nights. A different kind of Friday night. The Reades were given the box featured, in acknowledgement of the convenience of their house. Some tentative purchasing queries ensued.

Starting early the next day, Beatrice attempted preparations to cook a dish of precious rationed meat, and a rice pudding, in the manner demonstrated. When prepared, close down the lid and leave it for the day, so the agreeable woman had conclusively said. The exercise was not a success.

Disheartened after some further failures, Beatrice desisted.

'I lack the aptitude,' regretfully she said.

A librarian, she liked anything to do with books, to go to lectures on thought-provoking subjects—this was how she had met Penn Reade in Edinburgh— to listen to matters threshed out in the Friday circle. Since marrying, she appeared also to have given much time to the home. It was to be felt she did it in a dedicated way. She told Una she was happiest doing it, even if she was not a good cook. A local girl with a flair came each day to cook the main meal. Having lived in the house since her long trek, Una had come to think that Beatrice Reade's chief gift was a quiet strength. It was a catalyst, she felt, unobtrusively effecting a balance between the dynamic forces of her husband, the reactionary conventionality of her daughter, Madeline. Why, with what surely were enlightened parents, was Madeline reactionary?

And it was strange, it was ridiculous that, for Una Normile, such a place as the Reade's house was necessary. But, without demur, she had listened to what the solicitor had said. He was grave, composed, dark-suited. A Quaker, Penn Reade said. Not at all like the smart-alec would-be solicitors in the Law School Jack and Thady Keane had sometimes caricatured. He counselled that Una should stay in that one secure place which Mr Reade—he bent his head once in courtesy to Penn Reade—and his family made possible. He further counselled Miss Normile should not go anywhere alone outside the house. The Legion of Mary were by now afoot, as were priests and nuns of different orders. Already this had been made clear from the callers on Mr Forterre: people on a mission of persuasion and retrieval. It was amply evident, he continued, with just the faintest stir of a twinkle, that the hierarchy had been alerted to a stray from the fold.

While inside the walls of the Reade house, Una believed herself capable of resisting persuaders, but she also felt vulnerable should she venture beyond the walls. In danger of being swept off by well-doers, sincere in their conviction of acting for her redemption since, as they saw her, she was virtually standing in the flames of hell. While advising her not to go out without a companion, the solicitor said it was advisable policy to remain available, inside, to visitors. This foreguarded against accusations of enforced retention, of captivation on the the part of Mr Reade and his household.

Jack came. Angrier than ever in their furious youth.

'A turncoat. The worst day you ever were, I never thought you'd be that. I'll swing yet for an Englishman. I'm warning you.'

He slammed out of the house when he found she remained intractable. Nuns came twice, a priest three times. Succeeding them came a leading figure in the Legion of Mary. Each had intimated further visits. All of these encounters she had found very difficult to handle. She found the only way she could manage to meet them was with a wooden stubbornness. Argument was useless. She said very little. Afterwards, when they had gone, she felt drained. She dreaded any more visits. Above all, she dreaded that Minnie and Sean should come again. As it was, so many powerful things in their favour wrestled every day within her against her tie to Nelson. The mighty things of nineteen years against the momentous things of five months. The conflict was exhausting.

But Sean and Minnie did not come.

'I shouldn't keep saying it but here I am saying it again. I don't like having to be here. I don't like having to be confined to the limits of the Reade household.'

They sat on the edge of the narrow bed. The few shelves were full of books. Books were in little piles about their feet on the floor. He just sat there, head down, stroking her blue legs. Stockings she had none: not enough ration coupons nor money to get any. She had resigned from her civil service post; this had to be done if she were to keep lying low indefinitely. There were prices to pay for the illogic of constancy.

'No useful little salary. No Trinity—after all the planning. But I'm certainly learning. Not the sort of programme I ever envisaged. But I'm truly glad of the books.'

'Penn Reade has always been generous with books.'

'Very generous. They give me anything possible, he and Beatrice. One name leads to another: Westermark, Frazer, Havelock Ellis, Freud, Jung, Adler...more to come. Such a range. The reading, *it* makes things bearable, keeps me...going. For I really don't want to be here, Nelson. I've never had to be in such a...an...abject position. I'm not going to beg for stockings.'

She sprang off the bed and flung out both arms; her fingertips almost touched the walls either side, so narrow was the place where she slept.

'Oh and oh...for the wide wide *reidh* in Balnahown, for the Featherbed as it was in summer!'

'I know. Don't you think that of course I know how you feel? But what's to be done? What else for the present? Penn and Beatrice are decent, giving the refuge at all. Gladys Peach-Orr has offered a bed.'

'I know. She seemed to mean it too.'

'Clever at her work. Not too reliable outside of it—changes of mood.'

'She has been pleasant always to me. Glamour and kindness, I didn't think they'd go together.'

'But do you think you would feel any better with her? There is a big difference between knowing someone socially and having to live with that someone day to day. '

'I'm finding out plenty about that anyway, here. Things in myself that don't make it easier.'

'And the bed in Gladys's?'

'I don't think it would be any better there. Her place is very small; I don't see how we could be otherwise than on top of each other. Also, I'd have to be taking charity, as it's called, with Gladys also. That's what I'm doing here, taking charity from the Reades. To try to make some return I tackle the mending of sheets, tablecloths, darning. I take up ashes, make the fire, do wash-ups. But I tell you it rankles. I am as Maggie is in Balnahown. For the first time, I have a bit of fellow-feeling for Maggie. Do you remember Penn saying one Friday evening that service is one of the higher virtues? He was talking of "those who freely serve". I am not one of them. I had already thought a lot about all that in the days in Marymount. I decided then I was not of the stuff. Madeline tries to make me feel an object of alms.'

'But Beatrice? Surely not?'

'No, Beatrice does not. She would not.'

'My father lays himself open to scroungers,' Madeline had said.

'Madeline!' the cousins had exclaimed at her. 'We do not scrounge. Very well you know the arrangement.' A necessarily small sum from their trust fund to Penn Reade; after their qualification they would continue to repay.

'I was not referring to you. Many people use my father. He lets them. Likes to be the open-hearted philanthropist.'

'You are trying to get at me, Madeline, aren't you? You are succeeding,' Una said. 'I don't want this either, being here like this. I do not want to be an added expense to this household. I try...'

'Yes, you mend things.' Madeline was looking at a patch on the tablecloth she was putting away. It was not a well-done patch.

'I should do these repair jobs, Nelson, with a...with a...shining grace. I don't. I do them with poor grace. My patching is a depressed mess. I deserve the curl of the lip. But...oh but...I feel constricted here, resentful of the constraints. You know how I love the wide spaces, how I've thought of my family as a leading one in our remote Balnahown. I'm not a body to take Madeline's—or anyone's—high and mightiness and grudging.'

He was patting her shoulder and nodding, while seeming to be closely looking at his shabby shoes.

'Madeline does know the situation. Why it is I am as it were dumped here—the nuns, priests and all that. She has no use for any of it. She doesn't see why she should indulge me on that account. And as regards the mending, well, I've just told you about that. But she also says the whole business—meaning you, me, churches, Catholics, Protestants et cetera—is such a jungle, all of it.'

'She would.'

'And she's right—up to a point anyway. Furthermore, she says it is a great mistake for people to imagine that mixing the creeds, as she puts it, could work.'

'Oh yes, I know well how Madeline thinks.'

'She impresses on me how well she has planned her future.'

'Yes, yes. The tidy future of Madeline. Only time will tell.'

'You sound as if you almost wished time would tell an unhappy story for her.'

'No, not that. Quite wrong. Just you try to take no notice of her. Try not to, anyway.'

'I'm quite sure she fancies you.'

'You are?'

'I'm not gullible, Nelson. Don't pretend. To me it's plain, yes. In spite of Giles and the tidy future.'

'What she'd probably fancy is to boss me—boss me away from her father into an exemplary pattern of her dictation. Anyway all in the realms of fantasy—and in this present moment of reality I want you to cheer up. You are too down about things today. By the way, here is the weekly half-crown. Marvellous, isn't it?'

The raillery tended to bleakness. In a way, it was marvellous, for he could barely spare it. As she was fed and found in the Reade's house, she was putting the weekly half-crown towards buying a large roomy coat. Beatrice was to go with her.

'And Beatrice never complains when I come here to my burrow to read instead of getting on with the mending. Although no one makes me feel it, except Madeline, I am, of course, an awkwardness in the household. But in my more positive times, I see all this as part of my learning. There are the books, the Friday night talking and then the practical living out of matters—or attempting that anyway. I'm here—incarcerated, more or less until anyone might have time to go out with me. So I'm finding out more about the things in people—myself included—which can ferment in close-up daily living—more than when I had to stay in Neary's or in boarding school. All the petty petty frustrations, frictions, sensitivities about whose is what—territory, I suppose—oddities, idiosyncrasies. I feel I am a feeble creature, poor in the qualities required for generous cooperation. I ought not complain. In her place, I don't think I'd be any different from Madeline.'

Twenty-four

In the last weeks before his finals Nelson had stopped doing freelance articles. He had also asked for three weeks off from the part-time office work. He had said to the printing company that he would be glad to have the work again for some further short period after the exams. Until he moved on to the next phase, he had said. Perhaps to the employers he sounded somewhat enigmatic. They did not enquire as to the exact meaning but when the finals were over, they needed him no longer. Staff had had to be reduced off, they explained, business was slow; they were regretful but, naturally, part-time employees had to be the first to go.

'Too bad, Una. The three pounds a week were very necessary. And now...the next phase...there has to be an interim...'

'Yes?'

'Let me try to explain...

'Tell me first, are you glad you did the thing—the course in Trinity? Was it worth putting the four years into it?'

'Of course I'm glad. Entirely so. It's been useful in a lot of ways. To have done it while keeping up the analysis with Penn worked ultimately well for me. As you know now, the people in Trinity have had another view. I never discussed with any of them the fact that I was undergoing analysis—I felt no common ground in that respect. But, constantly, I have had opportuniies to compare, to evaluate academic approaches alongside Penn Reade's quite different way. Some people, of course, for whom gossip is the bread of life, put two and two together. Mrs Riverdale was quick at that.'

'But you're glad?'

'Yes, no doubt of it, I am glad. I wasn't quite sure how I might put the degree to use and now I will not be using it in quite the ways I variously thought about—Divinity for one and so on. It was good, though, that I was able to keep everything going—coursework, journalism, the part-time thing and analysis.'

'And now?'

'And now, as I say, an interim—a small one it will be—until a further matter gets sorted out.'

'Yet a further matter?'

'Well this has been with me, I suppose, ever since I began to think over Penn's attitude to life. I think since then I've been bit by bit gravitating to what could be called a…ministering—not the Church of Ireland, as I've found out. Recent developments make me believe it will not be that nor in any formal Church. In the meantime there will have to be…the dole…'

'Oh Nelson! Oh No! What are you talking about?'

'A short dole. I promise—I can still squeeze in the odd article and theatre review. They'll help. Be of cheer.'

'What do you mean, squeeze in? Won't you have a lot extra time now that you do not have to study?'

'I think I'll always have to study—in some form. There will always be a great deal of reading I want to do. New material keeps coming. And as to work, I'll be giving most of my time to the…I intend to embark on…'

He paused so long she had to ask, 'On what?'

'It could be called different names—I called it a ministering a minute ago. I don't know if I like the word minister, too much black suit going with it, grey suit, unbending necks in unbending dog collars. dogmas, dicta of rectitude. But ministering. Yes. How about chiropody?'

Not waiting for anything from her, still jocular, he continued, 'The whole of creation groaneth and travailleth because of corns, ingrown toenails, callouses. How will presidents, prime ministers, generalissimos manage if theirs are not seen to? Not to talk of the man in the street. It is he who will mainly be my concern, Una.'

He looked full at her.

'Revolting! Why do you have to put it that way? I don't want to think about those images. Especially now.'

'Chiropody, keeping sewers, dealing with refuse, unhealthy parts—someone has to do it.'

'What are you trying to say? Couldn't you put whatever it is differently? I hate those images. They don't suit the child. They make me queasy. You say I'm to cheer up and then you start on all those nauseating ideas.'

'You're quite right. Sorry, sorry. Especially as what I'm really trying to get across has to do with helping...'

'Helping?'

'Well, yes. Trying to. Trying to help. Work towards healing—if I can. I intend that to be what I do for the rest of my life. I know what it is to be lame. I've been lame for most of my life. It seems to me I have begun to walk with any kind of balance only very lately. It was Penn Reade who helped me to do that. I've had six years analysis by now. I am a very late walker. My mother and others in the family would call it something else—and a lot of other people besides.'

She remained silent. Since meeting him she had heard him say many times, 'Let's keep an open mind'. After minutes she said herself now, 'I'm keeping an open mind.'

'Agreed. It's what I've been trying to do all along—it's why I have chopped and changed as my mother—very understandably—so often called my doings. It's why I came to Ireland where Penn Reade was based, took up the study of psychoanalysis, went to Trinity, decided against the Divinity School—it is a pompous sounding name, isn't it?. Against turning RC. It seems to me now that this latest decision is what I've been keeping it open for...and after this, I'll still hope not ever to close it.'

'This is what it's all been coming to? Going the way of Penn Reade, always with an open mind?'

'Yes, in spite of the battles I've had with him. It could even be said, because of them. They were necessary. We didn't break on them. Ground had to be cleared. I have found him to be, after so much working through, the best guide—so far. And I have searched a great deal.'

'You've met all sorts of people.'

'I've mixed with a fair amount, yes. All callings.'

'Have worked at many levels.'

'True.'

'You've read, tried yourself out—from salesman to soldier to journalist to university man, clergyman-in-the making as Madeline put it...and to try to do what Penn Reade does, this is what, after all those other things, you want?'

'Yes. It's not what people in this country will have

expected of me, people to whom I came with introductions, Lady Duncarty et cetera, and other people besides—yours, mine. It goes counter to fashions in Trinity, the cynics, wits. Although in Trinity also are people who have been in every way helpful to me. They, too, will not like what I'm now going to do. It lays me wide to the scorn Madeline and many more show her father. But whatever is said, however much he is derided, Penn Reade does help, has healed—troubled people, people who have felt themselves fractured, maimed. Of those, I was one. I believe a great many people, a great many of us all, are that way in varying degrees—some of the time, most of the time, depending. You know it, too, I think. And you have told me about the Whelans, Proinsias de Burca, his wife and child, Mother Immaculata....many...it goes on..'

Penn Reade said, 'I advised him against it, Una. I didn't inveigle him. Rather the opposite. I've actually tried putting him off doing what I have done. It's a hard way to go, to remain proof against the pressures that demand official courses and the stamp of institutions, orthodoxy, after your name. Beatrice has always been with me in it all but you know yourself Madeline has not, I am often an embarrassment to her. There are prices to pay for not following the accepted channels. It will not be easy for Nelson, nor for you. Are you prepared for this, to go along with him, even so?'

'I am.'

Was she?

'To reject the establishment in any of its entrenched structures, so as to search out other more open values, is to be at risk. Nothing materially guaranteed. Sounds grandiloquent, a bit, doesn't it?' Nelson said.

She nodded. Then she said, 'But, quite simply, we are together in it.'

She had had those fantasies: Una Normile, highly paid, valued civil servant, holidaying on golden sands, all blemishes removed at the hands of costly beauticians; Una Normile, seductive in the most daring beach attire, object of female envy, of male desire.

She has now the reality: Una Normile, still in full possession of all blemishes, jobless, cut off from family—Sean, Minnie, Jack—from friends, the university course so wished for and finally with anxious negotiation, arranged. Walled-up—it could be seen as that—seen as a nuisance—not without some justification—by the daughter of the house which at present is spoken of as her safe place. She does not like any of it.

She need not be in this situation. The outlandishness of it all could have been avoided. She had choices. She need never have taken up with Nelson Forterre. She could have spared her deserving parents by upgrading herself in the civil service, even becoming a high-powered spinster senior officer, or if not that, contriving to become engaged to a conforming sexually contained male colleague of steady suburban tendencies and prospects.

With little or no tangible foundation, Nelson has promised to build shelters for her head.

He, too, had choices. Many. Women, career possibilities. He could now be a high earner, even married to the heiress his mother—joking in earnest

—begged for. Instead, he can afford to give her just a half-crown each week—in fact, down to two shillings this week. He has nothing to wear but cast-offs from his previous life.

He has said many things of a romantic nature. 'Ours was a bed of leaves. We were wedded in the leaves,' he said when she told him she was pregnant.

She responded in kind. 'Yes, we have pledged ourselves.'

They talked like this under autumn skies, looking out over the Irish Sea. When he could, he took her outside the house for fresh air along the piers.

Two days later he said, 'We should make it legal, Una, don't you agree?'

'I do, indeed I do…but…'

'Now that there is the baby, it would be best. The fact of a marriage certificate might also mean you would not be so vulnerable, could maybe move around again.'

'But I am under-age…how is marrying to happen? How can everything become legal? How do we go about it with no parental consent?'

'There are ways…I've been enquiring. The church off the quays—it's in the guide I once put together—you've been there with me, remember?'

'Ah yes, the mummies …'

'Yes. Mummies in the crypts and mummy-to-be before the altar…shh, say nothing, pathetic I know…'

'I said nothing but it is feeble. You could do better. It's not what's bothering me now, though. Tell me more about what has to be done.'

'The rector there would do it. Banns will have to be posted. No one knows us in that part of the city, so banns need not be a worry, I think. Will probably go unnoticed. Only they must go up, to have it right.

Also, I must be legally a resident of the parish. I must—to make this possible- sleep somewhere there for twenty-one consecutive nights. And I have found a place. A kip of a commercial hotel, the only thing I can afford. Cheapest rates mean three to a room. Washing facilities quite awfully primitive. In spite of all the throwing out of received ideas I've done, I still like a good wash—namby-pamby or else commendably sensible. whichever you like. That can be managed, too. Elsewhere—Tara Street baths or…we'll see.'

'How will we live, Nelson?'

'We will. You'll see. I absolutely believe it.'

'But…for example…a bed…a double bed…a room …How? Where?'

'We'll arrange to talk to Beatrice and Penn. About the work I hope to do. And other things.'

To talk to them together had to be arranged, even though you were under the same roof. With only brief breaks, Penn Reade worked continuously from early morning until, often, late evening.

'Yes,' Penn Reade said, 'it is true that I have to refuse people, that more than I can manage ask for therapy. It's also true that a point is arrived at when I am sure you, who have been studying with me those years, seriously studying and going deeply into the subject, are ready to do this work if you want to. And you say, categorically, you do want to. I have emphasised that I do not recommend your going the way I did: people expect the seal of orthodoxy. In my own case, I have been mostly able to deal with that expectation where I've encountered it. There has been the mudslinging. Being called quack and charlatan. I have been able to meet it because I know I am not offering inferior goods. I have undergone the essential process—analysis—abroad with an analyst of world repute. Have thoroughly covered the material, keeping up to date. Primarily, though, I have wished to work this way to—putting it simply—to help. All this you know. And then, too, I am tough, can take it. Not been easy. Not for Beatrice either, nor for Madeline. Madeline would have liked to see me in striped trousers, set up in Fitzwilliam Square or in one of the mental hospitals, prescribing shock treatment, frontal lobotomy, drugs, endless sedations. If I achieved results, helped some people get on with life, that is my only proof, justification. This is not a money game. Often people cannot pay. There are times when I make only a token charge, a penny a time. But a charge is necessary, part of the process. All this you also know very well. I have told Una it's a hard way.'

Una nodded.

Twenty-five

'We won't need any of it, Giles and I,' Madeline said. 'The auctioneers will come for most of it.'

She was referring to various objects of a domestic character which had been stored in the garden annex, filling it to the door. Her aunt, Beatrice's older sister had bequeathed these to her.

It was a December day; a thickening fog was advancing from the direction of the harbour. The horn sounded its warning: two carrying groans every minute or so. They stood in the only space left inside the entry. Madeline clutched a large woollen scarf across her chest with one hand, with the other she poked at a rolled-up mattress.

'And you can have the bed, too. What do you think of that, Nelson?'

'Very generous of you.'

'I don't think so. It's no favour. The mattress feels reasonable enough. And it is clean. My aunt was spotless.'

'Doubtless. Like her niece.'

'There's an undertone there, Nelson, I don't like.'

Sometimes there was this kind of peripheral banter between them. A play, at distance. Witnessing it, Una felt blades sharpening inside her.

'Anyway,' Madeline continued, 'it's my wedding present to you. To you both.' She laughed to include Una. A rich sound. A contrast to her spare orderly handsomeness. 'Times are hard.'

'They are,' Una said. 'Thank you.'

She was not going to effuse.

It had been settled that the annex would be their rented room once the auctioneers had more or less denuded it. Replete, it would seem, with a disdainful satisfaction in the prospect of her impending adequate equipping, when established as Giles's spouse, Madeline threw in a some extra pieces along with the bed. A sewing-machine was one of these. The sight of it brought a spontaneous Thanks! from Una. She would reform, practise the skill. There was to be much need of it.

Nelson and she would do whatever possible to redecorate the place at minimal cost. There was no heating; they would buy more hot water bottles. The leather suitcases with Forterre stamped on them which had resided under Nelson's bed in Trinity would have their potential put to use: Una was to look to herself, put full heart now into the business of sewing, turning to practical account stitching learnt in Marymount, to fashion a padded patchwork quilt out of Forterre cast-offs. They would make every effort to conserve any small warmth generated, pertinently arranging hangings to combat draughts and so on. What had been Una's cubicle was now to be Nelson's workroom, when given a new coat of paint and certain adjustments. A financial arrangement had been agreed with the Reades. In a manner of speaking, these moves signified aspects of the shelters Nelson repeatedly affirmed he would build for her head.

'One day,' he said, 'I'll take you around Europe on the best four wheels we can manage—all the places I've been and new ones.' She believed him.

She too had said to him, 'I love you' because—

because what? One reason was he had melted her. They flowed together. And thereafter she conceived. They had planned otherwise—no early conception— but the planning did not work. 'You are an Earth Goddess,' he said when she told him.

And what was this love? A feeling? That she certainly had. But were there not many aspects to love? Feeling, alone, was not enough. So much to think out, to learn. Love was difficult. But even so it seemed the most worthwhile of things. She had listened to Penn Reade, often disliking what he said. Monogamy could be selfish, this he had said. Not in the general Friday circle but only when a few well-tried friends were there with him and Beatrice. Nelson was one of these and, by virtue of him, Una was present. There was an air of particular seriousness. She shrank away from the hearing of it but she realised by now that no more should the mind be sealed up as in the previous years so much of it had to be. Blocked. Thoughts, ideas forbidden were from now to have the right of utterance, the right to be examined. Censorship was henceforth not to be part of her life. Courage, in this regard, had to be helped to grow. Innate curiosity had been a strong force in bringing her this far; curiosity without courage was idle.

We needed to keep discovering about love, Penn Reade said. He believed it to be a far wider thing, much more demanding than the first flush between people. It concerned itself with all people, not just lovers, with the nature of jealousy, with murderous rages, the urge to kill, how to confront and contain these titanic forces in the self, how to transform into constructive ways the energy that otherwise meant flooding blood and destruction. It had to do with giving. Forgiving.

The murder of Mary Ellen Whelan was still vivid. She thought about murders in Shakespeare, in history, the multiple murders of the ongoing war. Herself and Jack, love and hate imbalanced between them. Jack had said he would swing for an Englishman.

Beatrice Reade had quietly endorsed what her husband had said. Her eyes were down, something seeming to shadow her. There had once been a marital foursome which had only partially worked. There had been other relationships. Penn Reade and his wife were frank about these matters if approached in a climate of genuineness. Otherwise they were reserved.

'It is not a matter of playing around.' The couple supported each other.

Sometimes Una wished that she had not heard Penn Reade. Yet if Nelson had not first heard him, it was unlikely he and she would have gone thus far together. Their utterly different roots would have surely governed their adult growing in quite disparate ways.

Because she was a questioner, she would constantly question. Possibly quarrel, often and bitterly. But there were also the shelters he had promised. She had come to think that 'shelters for your head' meant, more than anything, abidingness. She trusted him in this promise because she found him constant in a search for what he believed to be the best. Because he was older, had travelled, knew so much of life unknown to her. She, with her lank hair, sallow skin, poor eyesight and other weaknesses, was promised cherishing in his wider capacity. Was she loving more than him the promise of this abiding cherishing?

Women liked Nelson. There would be other women. She could kill. She knew with sudden full certainty, that she had it in her to kill any woman who might seem to threaten Nelson's emollient devotion to herself. This devotion in no way blinded him. He had full awareness of the beauty of all women.

There would also be other men. She might want to prove herself further. In the tangles ahead, to give, to abide would be of paramount importance. For both of them. Also laughing.

It would come again, the laughing, surely? There had been a lot in the early summer.

Since the ride from Balnahown, Una had written home twice. In the first letter she tried hard to explain herself. She did not say in the customary way that she hoped they were well; to do so would be an impertinence. Minnie and Sean sent a reply each, sep- arately posted. The mere fact that Sean had brought himself to the point of composing a letter emphasised the gravity for him of the crisis she had brought about. He underlined how low in health her mother and he were, how severely under strain, as a result of her renegade sinful behaviour. Minnie's letter had the same content if differently expressed.

Once again Una had written, this time a pinched letter, since she felt the uselessness of trying to reach through to their understanding, to convince them that she loved them as always but really did believe she had to act otherwise than they wished. She could not speak of her pregnancy nor the coming marriage. To do it would compound their grief: her pregnancy before marriage was a spiritual death-knell, a scandal, a base sluttish crime. To be married in a Protestant church was not to be married at all. A Roman Catholic in her fallen condition, doing such a thing, was repeating, making more heinous the grossness of the first sin.

Every month Nelson had sent his mother a small tin of Bewley's shortbread. She wrote thanking him and complained only a very little about the cold, the inevitable lack of certain amenities in her wartime Cornish nook. The use of the word nook intimated, she knew, a certain reassurance, it conveyed a sense of her feeling protected. She wished to appear positive. She did not know what to make of him, marrying this peniless ingénue of rural Ireland brought up in the Church of Rome. He had always been a puzzle. Awkward. Even an embarrassment. These things she refrained this time from saying.

Nelson wore his navy blue suit, passed on years ago from a relative. It was in reasonable shape since he rarely wore it, disliking what he called formal get-up. Penn Reade was to give her away. No bridesmaid. Beatrice to act as matron of honour. Beyond this there were to be just the brief formalities of the service.

All four of them took the tram as far as they could and walked the rest of the way to the church. Afterwards they were to see the Tyrone Power film at the Metropole and then eat a meal of steak in Wynne's Hotel. These unleashed activities were arranged and covered courtesy of the Reades.

Penn Reade said, 'Well, Nelson, what would your people say to all of this today?'

'Very plebby.'

'No heiress, no restoration of family fortune?'

They laughed but behind the laugh Nelson Forterre wished for the impossible: his mother's warm presence and wishes. Una had yet to meet her. To meet the sister who had written to enquire whether she whom he proposed to marry was 'one of us, or of the lower orders'.

In her wartime dun tent-like coat, bought with savings from the half-crown per week, Una Normile longed for Minnie and Sean to be there near her with all their hearts. She wished for Jack, for her friends who used to be in the Craobh.

Nelson Forterre and Una Normile knew their choice meant, most likely, to be poor. It meant estrangement from family, the bafflement of many in their regard, lack of welcome in many circles.

Now they had come from the church. The ring was on her finger.

'And she is an heiress. And we will enrich—if not in the way my mother meant.'

Underneath in the dry vaults had lain the centuries-old mummies with their secrets. Indifferent, shrunken. Sublime in their brown dusty silence which embraced estrangement, reconciliation.

XV